ADVANCED LISTENING COMPREHENSION

Developing Aural and Notetaking Skills

Third Edition

Patricia Dunkel
Professor Emerita
Georgia State University

Frank Pialorsi
Professor Emeritus
University of Arizona

HEINLE
CENGAGE Learning™

Australia • Brazil • Japan • Korea • Mexico • Singapore • Spain • United Kingdom • United States

Advanced Listening Comprehension: Developing Aural and Notetaking Skills, Third Edition
Patricia Dunkel, Frank Pialorsi

Publisher, Adult and Academic ESL:
James W. Brown

Sr. Acquisitions Editor: Sherrise Roehr

Director of ESL and ELT Product Development:
Anita Raducanu

Development Editor: Kasia Zagorski

Director of Marketing: Amy Mabley

Technology Manager: Andrew Christensen

Production Manager: Sarah Cogliano

Manufacturing Manager: Marcia Locke

Project Coordination and Composition:
Pre-Press Company, Inc.

Cover Art: "Rhythme, joie de vivre," 1930 by
Robert Delaunay, © L & M SERVICES B.V.
Amsterdam 20040503. Photo: Philippe Migeat.
Musee National d'Art Moderne, Centre Georges
Pompidou, Paris, France © CNAC/MNAM/Dist.
Reunion des Musees Nationaux/Art Resource, NY.

Photo Manager: Sheri Blaney

Photo Researcher: Billie Porter

Cover Designer: Ha Nguyen

Text Designer: Carol Rose

For product information and technology assistance, contact us at
Cengage Learning Customer & Sales Support, 1-800-354-9706
For permission to use material from this text or product,
submit all requests online at **cengage.com/permissions**
Further permissions questions can be emailed to
permissionrequest@cengage.com

Library of Congress Control Number: 2004105951

ISBN 13: 978-1-4130-0396-3

ISBN 10: 1-4130-0396-6

Heinle
25 Thomson Place
Boston, MA 02210
USA

Cengage Learning is a leading provider of customized learning solutions with office locations around the globe, including Singapore, the United Kingdom, Australia, Mexico, Brazil, and Japan. Locate our local office at:
international.cengage.com/region

Cengage Learning products are represented in Canada
by Nelson Education, Ltd.

Visit Heinle online at **elt.heinle.com**
Visit our corporate website at **cengage.com**

Printed in the United States of America
8 9 10 11 12 13 15 14 13 12 11

Contents

To The Teacher

Advanced Listening Comprehension, Third Edition is a complete listening and notetaking skills program for advanced level students of English as a second or foreign language. Lectures and readings on topics of universal interest in the fields of Anthropology, History, Sociology, Communication, and Biology provide stimulating, content-based springboards for developing comprehension, notetaking, and academic study skills.

Advanced Listening Comprehension, Third Edition is one in a series of academic listening and notetaking publications. The complete program has been designed to meet the needs of students from the intermediate through the advanced levels and includes the following:

Intermediate Listening Comprehension......intermediate
Noteworthy..high intermediate
Advanced Listening Comprehension..........advanced

⬛ A new feature added to the third edition of *Advanced Listening Comprehension* is a video component. The orientation lecture for each chapter is now available on DVD or VHS. The video is meant to be used as a complement to the traditional audio program. Students may opt to view the orientation listening of a chapter on video in order to simulate a more authentic classroom listening and notetaking experience.

Pedagogical Overview

I. Research on the Effect of Notetaking on Lecture Learning, and Learners' Beliefs about the Usefulness of Notetaking

In a study of 234 English as a second language (ESL) learners at four universities in the United States about the importance of taking notes as they listened to TOEFL-like lectures in English, Carrell, Dunkel, and Mollaun (2002) reported that students' responses suggest that the learners: (1) felt a level of comfort and ease from being allowed to take notes while listening to lectures, (2) believed notetaking aided performance in answering questions about the lectures, and (3) judged that their recall of information was positively influenced by being allowed to take notes. In fact, 67 percent agreed that notetaking helped them answer the questions better than if they were not allowed to take notes; 75 percent agreed that notetaking made it easier to remember the information from the lecture; and 63 percent felt more at ease when they were allowed to take notes during lecture learning. In addition, the researchers found that those who listened and took notes on mini-lectures in the arts and humanities did better on an information-recall test than those who were not allowed to take notes. Although much more research needs to be done on the effect of notetaking on lecture learning, the research by Carrell, Dunkel, and Mollaun does suggest that notetaking is an important strategy that ESL learners need to acquire if they are going to be asked to listen to and absorb information from lecture-type speech.

II. Focus on Developing Academic Listening Comprehension Proficiency: Models of Noninteractive and Interactive Lectures

The lecture method of instruction pervades institutions of higher learning in North America and in many areas throughout the world. It is considered to be a cost-effective method of instruction and "the most dramatic way of presenting to the largest number of students a critical distillation of ideas and information on a subject in the shortest possible time" (Elsen, cited in Gage and Berliner, 1984, p. 454). Not only do many students encounter the lecture method of instruction during university life, but more and more students across the globe are experiencing lectures given in English. As Flowerdew (1994) observes, as a result of the spread of English as an international language, increasing numbers of people are studying at the university level through the medium of English, whether in their own country or in English-speaking countries as international students. He notes, further, that a major part of the university experience of these domestic and international students involves listening to lectures and developing academic listening skills. "Academic listening skills are thus an essential component of communicative competence in a university setting" (Flowerdew, 1994, p. 7).

Buck (2001), Dunkel (1995), Dunkel and Davis (1994), Flowerdew (1994), Mendelsohn and Rubin (1995), Richards (1983), and Rost (1990) have contributed a substantial amount of knowledge to the growing body of literature on what constitutes and fosters proficiency in academic listening, as well as conversational listening. In his scholarly book *Academic Listening: Research Perspectives*, Flowerdew, for example, identifies a number of the most distinctive features of academic listening, pointing out that one of the most significant features that distinguishes academic listening from conversational listening is the lack (or relatively rare use) of turn taking in academic listening. "In conversation, turn-taking is obviously essential, while in lectures turn-taking conventions will only be required if questions are allowed from the audience or come from the lecturer" (p. 11). As a result, the lecture listener may have to listen with concentration for long stretches of time without having the chance to take a turn to speak during the lecture presentation. In other words, the listener must develop the ability "to concentrate on and understand long stretches of talk without the opportunity of engaging in the facilitating functions of interactive discourse, such as asking for repetition, negotiating meaning, using repair strategies, etc." (Flowerdew, 1994, p. 11). Some lecture situations allow for little or no participation and interaction from the student-listener. This type of lecture is sometimes referred to as a "talk-and-chalk" or a noninteractive lecture. In the United States, students typically experience this type of lecture when attending classes held in large lecture halls containing large numbers of students, although the nonparticipatory lecture can (and often does) occur in nearly every instructional setting.

The noninteractive lecture situation is, however, not the only type of lecture experience that international students may have at a university where English is the only or dominant language of instruction. Some lecturers do adopt a more interactive lecturing style, particularly when they are lecturing to relatively small audiences, that is, of thirty or fewer students. The language of the more interactive lecturer requires that students engage in more conversational listening, and the language of the lecturer will generally contain some of the hallmarks and conventions of conversation, albeit of academic conversation. The lecturer, for example, may make allowance for (or encourage) questions from listeners seeking clarification of information heard or read in a reading assignment, or the lecturer may ask questions to check that the listeners understood bits of information and points made.

Advanced Listening Comprehension, Third Edition offers students models of both kinds of lectures: the noninteractive academic lecture and the slightly more interactive academic lecture. In addition, a third, more informal style of information presentation is offered. *Advanced Listening Comprehension, Third Edition* listeners are presented with three models of lecture discourse on the same topic. The first model exposes students to uninterrupted lecture discourse, similar to the kind heard in a large-audience, noninteractive "talk-and-chalk" lecture, or to a news broadcast heard on the radio. During this initial listening, the student listens to perceive or become familiar with the overall general structure and content of the lecture. While listening, the learner reviews a notetaking outline of the lecture, which outlines aspects of the content and structure of the information. With this initial listening experience, the listener is "oriented" toward the structure and content of the lecture, and he or she absorbs some background needed to support a more thorough understanding of the lecture. The second lecture presentation models a more slowly paced delivery of information; the lecture is interrupted by a mentor/guide who asks questions of the listener/notetaker and who attempts to assist with the task of taking notes on the lecture information. (The mentor highlights some of the main ideas, and reiterates many of the details so the listener can decide whether or not to encode the information in his or her notes.) The third exemplar models a more conversational syle (albeit a more academic conversational style), with the students paraphrasing and restructuring the information presented during the first and second lectures. The presentation includes hallmarks of more spontaneous speech, the kind used when delivering more "impromptu" lectures. The notetaker is then given the chance to become the lecturer and to recap the lecture from the notes taken on the lecture.

III. Focus on Developing Notetaking Skills: Providing Opportunity to Develop the Ability to Select and Encode Information in Notes

In addition to contrasting the difference in turn-taking conventions associated with academic and conversational styles discussed previously, Flowerdew (1994) points out that conversational and academic listening differ one from the other in terms of the listener's desire to take notes on the information heard. To do so, the listener needs to engage in a five-stage process: he or she must "decode, comprehend, identify main points, decide when to record these, write quickly and clearly" (Flowerdew, 1994, p. 11). Lecture notes are usually taken and stored in notebooks for study-and-review purposes. In their article titled "Second Language Listening Comprehension and Lecture Note-taking," Chaudron, Loschky, and Cook (1995) underscore the importance of this **external storage function** of lecture notes. The structure and format of *Advanced Listening Comprehension, Third Edition* reinforces the importance of this external storage function of the notes taken since the students must use the notes taken during the lectures to respond to short-answer and essay examination questions given several class sessions following delivery of the lecture. *Advanced Listening Comprehension, Third Edition* also gives students the chance to develop their individual notetaking approaches and styles, though it provides some guidance in the form of the notetaking mentor who interrupts the lecture to provide students with additional time to write down information, to fill in information missed, and to signal some of the major global ideas and details contained in the information heard.

IV. Focus on Developing General Communication Skills: Broadening the Base of Skill Development

Although development of academic listening comprehension proficiency and notetaking skills is the chief objective of the instructional program of *Advanced Listening Comprehension, Third Edition*, it is not the exclusive goal of the program. The authors recognize that advanced ESL students are not just "information sponges." They are much more than that. In addition to obtaining and absorbing information and knowledge, they also function as users and creators of information and knowledge. Furthermore, they react to information learned, often in discussion of issues with peers. In addition, during their university days, students not only *listen* to obtain and learn information, they also *read* to acquire information, and they discuss and react to the information gained via both their ears and eyes. Occasionally, they are expected to give oral reports in class and to participate in study groups (see Mason, 1994). Upon occasion, they are required to interact after class with their instructors, or if they are teaching assistants, to interact with their students. They commonly interact with their peers. A student might, for example, be asked by a peer who was absent from a lecture to provide him or her with a synopsis of the lecture or a summary of the reading assignment given by the professor. The students might also be asked to evaluate or to react to the information presented. *Advanced Listening Comprehension, Third Edition* seeks, therefore, to help students not only grasp, comprehend, and store information they have heard and read, but also to construct and share information through speaking and writing. It provides students an opportunity to read information related to (but not precisely the same as) the topics of the lectures, and it requires the learner to discuss issues in oral exchanges and/or written communication.

V. Summary Goals

In brief, the goals of *Advanced Listening Comprehension, Third Edition* are primarily threefold: (1) to help students build their academic listening comprehension proficiency in English, (2) to assist them in developing or improving their English-lecture notetaking skills; and (3) to enhance their ability to read and discuss information and issues related to the general and/or specific topics contained in the lectures heard. These goals are achieved, we trust, with the aid of the instructional design of the units and the eclectic approach outlined below.

The Instructional Design of Each Unit

I. **Chapters**
   A. **Proverbs and Wise Sayings** Students read proverbs and sayings to ponder and/or discuss general and specific meanings, as well as relevance.
   B. **Prelistening** Students read a short introduction to and synopsis of the focus and content of the information contained in the lecture.
   C. **Think About This** Students answer one or two questions to anticipate content and to share experiences and feelings evoked by the questions.
   D. **Types of Information Presentations and Delivery Styles** Students listen to three models of the lecture on the topic with different task requirements for each model.
   1. *The Orientation Listening Model:* Students get oriented to the structure and content of the lecture and build background knowledge (the lecture is scripted and representative of broadcast style).
   2. *The Listening and Notetaking Model:* Students listen to the lecture with mentoring support for notetaking (the lecture is scripted with elements of redundancy provided, and is given at a slightly slower speed than that of the Orientation Listening).

🎧 **3.** *Listening to a Recounting of the Lecture:* Students listen to a recounting of the lecture by a student; the notes taken by the listener can be checked for accuracy and completeness during the presentation; the style includes characteristics of more extemporaneous presentations, including use of redundancies, paraphrases, verbal fillers [for example, "uhmmm," "errr"] repetitions, corrections, and so forth in the speech).

    E. **Recapping the Lecture from Your Notes** Students recap the lecture from the notes they have taken.

    F. **Reading Expansion** Students read authentic material (for example, a newspaper article, a segment of a book, a research project, and so forth) on a related topic.

    G. **Discussing Information and Issues** Students discuss and react to the issues by responding to questions related to the topic.

    H. **Journal Writing** Students maintain a written journal in which they write about topics and issues of interest or concern to them.

    I. **Research Project** Students do research to find out more about the lecture topic or a related topic. They prepare a paper or presentation on the information that they find.

II. **Unit Exam**

    A. **Information Recognition/Recall Exam** Students answer short-answer questions and essay-type questions using the notes they took on the lecture. The storage function of the notes is emphasized in this component of the listening and notetaking program. Students are also asked to construct a number of test questions to give fellow students and peers. Students, thus, participate in test construction and information checking in individual ways.

References

Buck, F. (2001). *Assessing listening.* New York: Cambridge University Press.

Carrell, P., Dunkel, P., & Mollaun, P. (2002). *The effects of notetaking, lecture length and topic on the listening component of TOEFL 2000.* Princeton, NJ: Educational Testing Service.

Chaudron, C., Loschky, L. & Cook, J. (1994). Second language listening comprehension and lecture note-taking. In J. Flowerdew (Ed.), *Academic listening: Research perspectives* (pp. 75–92). New York: Cambridge University Press.

Dunkel, P. (1995). Authentic second/foreign language listening texts: Issues of definition, operationalization, and application. In P. Byrd, *Material writers' handbook.* Boston: Heinle & Heinle.

Dunkel, P., & Davis, J. (1994). The effects of rhetorical signaling cues on the recall of English lecture information by speakers of English as a native or second language. In J. Flowerdew (Ed.), *Academic listening: Research perspectives* (pp. 55–74). New York: Cambridge University Press.

Flowerdew, J. (Ed.). (1994). *Academic listening: Research perspectives.* New York: Cambridge University Press.

Gage, N. L., & Berliner, D. C. (1984). *Educational psychology* (3rd ed.) Boston: Houghton Mifflin.

Mason, A. (1994). By dint of: Student and lecturer perceptions of lecture comprehension strategies in first-term graduate study. In J. Flowerdew (Ed.), *Academic listening: Research perspectives* (pp. 199–218). New York: Cambridge University Press.

Mendelsohn, D., & Rubin, J. (Eds.). (1995). *A guide for the teaching of second language listening.* San Diego, CA: Dominie Press.

Richards, J. (1983). Listening comprehension: Approach, design, procedure. *TESOL Quarterly, 17,* 219–240.

Rost, M. (2002). *Teaching and researching listening.* New York: Longman.

Acknowledgements

The authors and publisher would like to thank the following reviewers:

Michael Berman
Montgomery College

Patricia Brenner
University of Washington

Jennifer Kraft
Oakland Community College

Lois Lundquist
Harper College

Marie Mitchell
Arizona State University

The authors would also like to acknowledge the critical assistance, the creative input, and the editorial support of Mr. Jim Brown, Publisher, Adult and Academic ESL, and Ms. Kasia Zagorski, Development Editor of Heinle Publishers. The third edition of *Advanced Listening Comprehension* is a better book, audio, and video program, thanks to their enormous help and good spirit.

Anthropology:
The Evolution of Human Endeavor

THINK ABOUT AND DISCUSS THE MEANING OF THE FOLLOWING QUOTATION:

If we are to achieve a richer culture, rich in contrasting values, we must recognize the whole gamut of human potential, and so weave a . . . fabric . . . in which each diverse human gift will find a fitting place.

—Margaret Mead (1901–1978)

American Anthropologist

1

Anthropology:
The Study of Human Beings and Their Creations

THINK ABOUT AND DISCUSS THE MEANINGS OF THE FOLLOWING QUOTATIONS:

The awe and dread with which the untutored savage contemplates his mother-in-law are amongst the most familiar facts of anthropology.

—Sir James George Frazer (1854–1941)

Scottish Anthropologist

Almost [all] of our actions and desires [are] bound up with the existence of other human beings.

—Albert Einstein (1879–1955)

American Theoretical Physicist

5. Why must culture and society coexist?

6. What is necessary for a society to share a single culture?

7. What is another term for *multicultural*?

8. Where do you find groups of subcultures?

9. List three universals common to all cultures.

10. According to Edward Sapir, why is the individual important? Do you agree?

Part Two: Essay Questions

Answer each essay question below in a paragraph. Use the notes that you took on the lectures to provide support for the claims you make in your essay.

1. When and where was the field of anthropology developed?

2. Explain physical anthropology. What is the goal of this field and how do physical anthropologists study it?

3. Explain cultural anthropology. What is the goal of this field and how do cultural anthropologists study it?

4. Which subfield of anthropology would you most like to work in? Why? What would you like to learn?

5. Explain how anthropology can help us plan for the future and solve human problems.

6. Explain the different ways that culture is defined in the lecture.

7. Is knowing the words of another language enough for meaningful communication? What else is needed?

8. Which of Seelye's six skills for intercultural communication do you think is the most important?

9. Give an example of a multicultural society. Why is it considered multicultural?

10. Think about the three universals common to all cultures. Choose one universal and explain why you think it is true for all cultures.

Part Three: Constructing Test Questions

Use the notes that you took on the lectures in Unit One to write three test questions about each lecture. After you write the questions, ask a classmate to use his or her notes to answer the questions.

History:
The Passing of Time and Civilizations

THINK ABOUT AND DISCUSS THE MEANING OF THE FOLLOWING QUOTATION:

Those who cannot remember the past are condemned to repeat it.

—George Santayana (1863–1952)

American philosopher and poet

The Egyptian Pyramids:
Houses of Eternity

THINK ABOUT AND DISCUSS THE MEANINGS OF THE FOLLOWING QUOTATIONS:

The average person does not know what to do with this life, yet wants another one which will last forever.

—Anatole France (1844–1924)

French writer

I don't want to achieve immortality through my work. . . . I want to achieve it through not dying.

—Woody Allen (1935–)

American filmmaker

I. PRELISTENING

A. Preview of the Content

The pyramids of ancient Egypt have fascinated and puzzled humanity for centuries. Just how were they built at a time when human beings lacked knowledge of advanced mathematics, when we had no modern machinery or technology, when we had only copper tools to work with? Certain other questions come to mind when trying to understand the incredible mystery of these fantastic monuments: questions such as why would someone—let's say a king—require that 100,000 workers labor for twenty years to construct a tomb to place his dead body in? Was it his attempt to secure immortal life for his soul when his body had stopped functioning? Was it his attempt to hide his possessions from robbers? Was it his fear of being forgotten—of being human rather than superhuman? Or was it his attempt to be equal to an immortal god? To all of these questions, the answer appears to be "yes, indeed."

In the presentation, the lecturer will trace the evolution and the development of the pyramids, and will attempt to show the human and religious significance of these gigantic monuments to mankind's search of immortality.

B. Think about This

What's the most interesting structure in the world? The Eiffel Tower? The Great Wall of China? A structure in your country? List three reasons why you find this structure interesting and share these reasons with a partner.

II. LISTENING

🎧 A. Orientation Listening

As you listen to the lecture for the first time, use the outline below to help you understand the general content of the lecture and the topics discussed. The outline should help you perceive the overall structure of the lecture and the main ideas presented by the lecturer.

I.   The pyramids of Egypt have survived time and weather.

II. The pyramids were constructed as burial places for the ancient Egyptian royal family members.
   A. The ancient Egyptians believed in life after death.
     1. They prepared for their afterlife by building tombs (pyramids) and collecting possessions to put into the tombs.
     2. They had their bodies preserved from decay by embalming.
     3. They believed that the dead person could take his or her earthly possessions along to the next world.
   B. The tombs were built to outsmart grave robbers, but almost all of the tombs were broken into and robbed.

III. The structure of the pyramids evolved over the centuries.
   A. The mastaba was constructed during the First and Second Dynasties (3100–2665 B.C.E.).
   B. The "step pyramid" (the "typical" pyramid) was built during the Third Dynasty (2664–2615 B.C.E.).
     1. Built for King Zoser by the architect Imhotep.
     2. Is a pile of mastabas.
     3. King Zoser's step pyramid was never covered with stone to give it a smooth surface.
   C. The pyramids of Giza were built during the Fourth Dynasty (2614–2502 B.C.E.).
     1. Located near the town of Giza, which is outside Cairo.
     2. The best preserved of all the pyramids.
       a. Khufu's (Cheops's) pyramid is the largest.
       b. Khafre's pyramid is smaller.
       c. Mankaure's pyramid is the smallest.

IV. The construction of pyramids declined after the Fourth Dynasty.
   A. Pyramids offered little or no protection for the dead kings and nobles and for their possessions from grave robbers.
   B. Thutmose I commanded an underground tomb be built far from the Nile River and Cairo (in the Valley of the Kings).
   C. Most pharaohs followed Thutmose's example.

B. Listening and Notetaking

Now that you've listened to the lecture once, listen to it again and take notes. The lecturer will present a slower-paced version of the lecture and will reiterate information so you will have time to take down the information in note form. You will be assisted in your notetaking by a notetaking mentor who will ask you to check that you wrote down important information.

C. Listening to a Recounting of the Lecture

Listen to a student recount the lecture. The student will speak in a more informal, spontaneous style, paraphrasing and summarizing the information in the lecture. As you listen, check to be sure that your notes are complete.

III. POSTLISTENING

A. Recapping the Lecture from Your Notes: Presenting the Information Orally

Recount the information you heard in the lecture to a partner, the class, or your teacher. Use your notes to help you relate the main ideas as well as the supporting information that you heard in the lecture.

B. Discussing Information and Issues Presented in the Lecture

In a group of two to four students, discuss the questions below. Your teacher may ask you to address one of the questions or all of them. During your discussion, use the information in your notes to support your ideas. At the end of the discussion, a representative from the group should summarize the group's discussion for the class.

1. Explain why King Thutmose I decided not to be buried in a pyramid. Why had the pharaohs before him built the pyramids? What other ways do you think the Egyptian pharaohs could have solved the problems they encountered with their system of burial?

2. The construction of pyramids was an example of the search for everlasting life. In what other ways have people searched for immortality? Why do you think people continue to search for immortality?

3. The lecturer comments that the pyramids are very puzzling monuments and that many questions and mysteries surround the Egyptian pyramids. As a group, make a list of the questions and mysteries that the lecturer mentioned; then add questions that your group has about the pyramids that were not answered in the lecture.

IV. READING EXPANSION

A. Reading a Magazine Article

The next passage is an excerpt from an article that appeared in *National Geographic* magazine. Before you read the passage, answer the following questions:

1. The following passage is about the Egyptian pharaoh Ramses II. Using the information about pharaohs from the lecture, write three statements you expect to be true about Ramses II. Then share your ideas with your classmates.

2. If you were going to write an article about the Egyptian pharaoh Ramses II, what would you want to find out? If you were writing an article for the general public, what information do you think would interest people?

3. In this unit's lecture, the speaker mentioned that the pharaohs were mummified. What do you remember about this technique for preserving bodies? If you could learn three more things about mummification, what would you want to find out? Share your ideas with a partner.

Ramses the Great

by Rick Gore

NATIONAL GEOGRAPHIC MAGAZINE, APRIL 1991

On my last day in Egypt I finally receive permission from the Egyptian Antiquities Organization to see Ramses' mummy. My colleague, Lou Mazzatenta, is also permitted to photograph the pharaoh. At the Egyptian Museum in Cairo, conservation director Nasry Iskander lifts the dark velvet off the mummy case. I behold the face. Browned and chisel sharp. Arms crossed regally across the chest. A long neck, a proud aquiline nose, and wisps of reddish hair, probably colored by his embalmers.

Ramses' mummification and burial rites likely took the traditional 70 days. Embalmers removed internal organs, placing the liver, lungs, stomach, and intestines in sacred jars. His heart was sealed in his body. Egyptians believed that it was the source of intellect as well as feeling and would be required for the final judgment. Only if a heart was as light as the feather of truth would the god Osiris receive its owner into the afterlife.

Egyptians did not appreciate the brain. The embalmers drew it out through the nose and threw it away.

After they dried the corpse with natron salt, the embalmers washed the body and coated it with preserving resins. Finally they wrapped it in hundreds of yards of linen.

Within 150 years of Ramses' burial, his tomb was robbed by thieves and his mummy desecrated. Twice reburied by priests, the body retained some of its secrets. X-ray examination of the body indicated that Ramses suffered badly from arthritis in the hip, which would have forced him to stoop. His teeth were severely worn, and he had dental abscesses and gum disease.

The photography finished, the velvet is replaced over Ramses' mummy—but the face stays with me. Not the face of Shelley's Ozymandias, not that of a god, but the face of a man. Was Ramses bombastic, cruel, ego driven? By our standards, certainly. He left no evidence of the human complexity or the bitterly learned insights that redeem such proudful mythic kings as Oedipus, or Shakespeare's King Lear, but he did love deeply and lose. And all those children who died before him—Ramses knew human suffering. Did he really believe he was a god? Who can say? But clearly, he strove to be the king his country expected—providing wealth and security—and succeeded. More than most, this man got what he wanted.

Reprinted with permission of the National Geographic Society.

B. Discussing Information and Issues Presented in the Reading

1. What surprised or interested you most about the mummification process described in the passage? Why? Tell a classmate.

2. How might someone in the future interpret today's burial customs? What do our burial customs say about our beliefs about the afterlife and immortality?

3. The article states that the Egyptians believed that the heart was the "source of intellect as well as feeling." Modern medicine credits the brain with being the source of intellect and Western tradition considers the heart to be the center of emotions and feelings. In English there are many proverbs that reinforce this understanding, such as: "Use your head" to mean think about something critically, and "His heart isn't in it," which is said about someone who does not really care emotionally about the task he must do. Where does your culture consider to be the center of human intellect? Where does your culture place the center of feeling and emotion? Is this modern understanding the same as it was many years before? Relate any proverbs from your language that reinforce this understanding of the origin of intellect and emotion.

4. The author states that Ramses II "strove to be the king his country expected—providing wealth and security—and succeeded." What do you expect from a leader of a country? Are your expectations similar to or different from the expectations listed by the author of the article? What qualities do you think are ideal in the leader of a country? Explain why.

Journal Writing

Respond to one of the following questions in your journal.

1. The construction of pyramids was an example of the search for life everlasting. Why and in what other ways have people searched for immortality?

2. Do you believe in an afterlife? Explain why or why not? Describe the factors (education, religion, family, schooling, and so on) that contributed to your belief.

Research Project

Individually or in a group, research one of the following topics. Write a short paper on the topic, or plan and present a group presentation to inform the class about the topic.

a. The discovery of the tomb of the boy pharaoh, King Tutankhamen.
b. Compare and contrast the mastaba pyramids with the step pyramids.
c. The pyramid of Cheops.
d. The workers who built the pyramids.
e. The pyramids of Mayan and Aztec culture in South America.
f. The life of Ramses II or another ancient Egyptian king or queen.
g. Another question that interests you or your group.

The First Emperor of China:
Building an Empire and a House of Eternity

THINK ABOUT AND DISCUSS THE MEANINGS OF THE FOLLOWING QUOTATIONS:

We live in a culture here in [Los Angeles] that believes, with enough trips to the gym and plastic surgery, death is something that can be denied or cheated.

—Lisa Takeuchi Cullen

Time magazine, July 2003

History is the version of past events that people have decided to agree upon.

—Napoleon

French emperor (1769–1821)

Pale death with impartial tread beats at the poor man's cottage door and at the palace of kings.

—Horace

Roman poet (65–8 B.C.E.)

I. PRELISTENING

A. Preview of the Content

The women's movement has become one of the most talked-about and important social movements of the twentieth century in the United States and in many other countries throughout the world. It has, for better or for worse, altered the course of American politics, education, and employment, and it has even changed the family structure. As a result, it has had a tremendous impact on the lives of millions of American men, women, and children. In this lecture we will be dealing primarily with the impact the women's movement has had on the political, economic, and social system of the United States, but this does not mean that its influence has not been felt in other countries. It certainly has been, and in all probability will be, felt in even more countries in the future.

The lecturer starts out by explaining the history of the women's movement since its beginnings in the 1800s. She covers most of the major social changes that occurred through the 1900s as well and then, in some detail, she discusses the progress that has been made in the present day. The lecturer explains changes in the areas of the workplace, politics, and the home that have occurred as a result of the women's movement, and she uses examples, illustrations, and statistics to back up her claims.

At the end of the lecture, the lecturer explains that although many people still consider the women's movement to be a necessary element of American society, many people have differing opinions about the form the movement should take. The lecturer concludes by stating that the terms associated with the women's movement are not nearly as important as the changes that the movement has caused in society, particularly in the United States.

B. Think about This

1. With a partner, describe **two** women you greatly admire and tell why you admire them. In what ways are the women similar? In what ways are they different?

2. Rank the following priorities in order of importance (1 = highest; 9 = lowest) for each woman: 1) motherhood and family, 2) professional career, 3) business success, 4) political ambition, 5) physical beauty, 6) intelligence, 7) wealth, 8) education, 9) you name the quality.

Woman's name _____   Woman's name _____

1. _____   1. _____
2. _____   2. _____
3. _____   3. _____
4. _____   4. _____
5. _____   5. _____
6. _____   6. _____
7. _____   7. _____
8. _____   8. _____
9. _____   9. _____

II. LISTENING

🎧 *A. Orientation Listening*

As you listen to the lecture for the first time, use the outline below to help you understand the general content of the lecture and the topics discussed. The outline should help you perceive the overall structure of the lecture and the main ideas presented by the lecturer.

I. The women's movement is a century and a half old
    A. Organized movement began in mid-1800s (Ryan: *Feminism and the Women's Movement)*
    B. Women then considered nonpersons and could not
        1. inherit property
        2. control their own money
        3. gain custody of their children after divorce
        4. vote

II. Changes in the 1900s—Europe and America
    A. After World War I, many countries gave women the right to vote (1920 in the U.S.)
    B. World War II—women entered the job market
    C. Today women have gained more job opportunities
        1. Hold positions of leadership
        2. Entering male-dominated professions: firefighters and pilots

III. Women-owned businesses
    A. Are one of fastest-growing segments of U.S. economy
        1. "Hot spots" for women entrepreneurs in western United States: Idaho, Wyoming, Utah, Nevada, Arizona
    B. Employ more people domestically than the Fortune 500 worldwide
    C. Challenge women to find balance between work, family, and social life

IV. Women in politics
    A. Number of female state legislators has grown more than 500 percent since 1969
    B. Countries that have had women presidents and prime ministers

V. The family
   A. Less than 10 percent of American families have traditional working father and stay-at-home mother
   B. Child care
      1. Men playing more active role
      2. Business and government helping
      3. More government-sponsored child care and parental leave are needed

VI. The women's movement and feminism
   A. Diverse opinions about how to achieve equality for men and women
   B. Feminism
      1. Difficult to define
      2. Everybody should have the opportunity to be the best they can (*Feminism and the Women's Movement*)

VII. The contributions to society by the women's movement and feminism
   A. Society is benefiting from these women's contributions
   B. Women have more freedoms, opportunities, and headaches

🎧 B. Listening and Notetaking

Now that you've listened to the lecture once, listen again and take notes on the information contained in the lecture. The lecturer will present a slower-paced version of the lecture and will reiterate information so you will have time to take down the information in note form. You will be assisted in your notetaking by a notetaking mentor who will ask you to check that you wrote down important information.

_____

_____

_____

_____

_____

_____

_____

_____

_____

_____

_____

_____

_____

_____

_____

_____

_____

_____

_____

_____

_____

_____

∩ C. Listening to a Recounting of the Lecture

Listen to a student recount the lecture. The student will speak in a more informal, spontaneous style, paraphrasing and summarizing the information from the lecture. As you listen, check to be sure that your notes are complete.

III. POSTLISTENING

A. Recapping the Lecture from Your Notes: Presenting the Information Orally

Recount the information you heard in the lecture to a partner, the class, or your teacher. Use your notes to help you relate the main ideas as well as the supporting information that you heard in the lecture.

B. Discussing Information and Issues Presented in the Lecture

In a group of two to four students, discuss the questions below. Your teacher may ask you to address one of the questions or all of them. During your discussion, use the information in your notes to support your ideas. At the end of the discussion, a representative from the group should summarize the group's discussion for the class.

1. Discuss the roles women play in your country in
    a. the home
    b. the economy and the job market
    c. politics
    d. religion
    e. education
    f. other areas

2. Should women who have children (ages newborn to teenagers) work outside the home? Provide at least five reasons why they should or should not.

3. Are there fields of employment that are particularly suitable for women? What are they? Are there certain fields that are particularly unsuitable for women? What are they? If you have listed any occupations as suitable or unsuitable for women, explain what aspects of these occupations you feel make the jobs suitable or unsuitable for women.

IV. READING EXPANSION

A. Reading a Newspaper Article

The lecture introduced you to some of the roles that women play in North American society and explained how these roles are changing. The information in the lecture, however, is rather specific to the United States. The article that you are about to read focuses on the women's movement in another country—Japan. Before you read the article, answer the questions below.

1. Read the title of the article. What does the title tell you about the women's movement in Japan? What do you think it means to be a "reluctant feminist"? Share ideas with your classmates.

2. According to the title of the article, the women's movement in Japan is not moving very fast. Why might this be so? With a partner, list three possible reasons. Then compare ideas with your classmates.

3. If you were going to write a newspaper article about the women's movement in Japan, what would you want to find out? Work with your classmates to write a list of questions. Then look for answers to your questions as you read the article.

Reluctant Feminists

Women's Movement in Corporate Japan Isn't Moving Very Fast

Government Pushes Hiring, But Female Professionals, Firms Stay Committed

Dorms, Curfews and Uniforms

Yumiko Ono
Staff Reporter
THE WALL STREET JOURNAL

Tokyo—Yuka Hashimoto was hired from college two years ago by Fuji Bank Ltd. and was assured she could rise as high in management as her talents allowed. She was assigned to the bond trading desk.

Now clad in a bright pink suit, she sometimes finds herself serving tea to office guests. Her male colleagues never do.

Though she privately complains that the task can interfere with her work, the 24-year-old Ms. Hashimoto gasps at any suggestion that she refuse the chore as sexist. "I'm not saying I won't serve tea because I'm a career-track employee," she says.

Like Ms. Hashimoto, many Japanese women are reluctant feminists. They generally accept the six biased slights common in Japanese companies. And when asked to choose between career and marriage, professional women more often choose to stay home. The women's movement here is moving nowhere fast.

"In America, women started a movement because they looked at the situation as a problem," says Eiko Shinotsuka, associate professor of home economics at Ochanomizu University, who follows women's labor issues. But in Japan, she says, "many women aren't particularly dissatisfied with the situation they're in."

Poll Results

In a recent survey by Phillip Morris K.K., the Japanese subsidiary of U.S.-based Phillip Morris Cos., 55% of 3,000 Japanese women polled said they weren't being treated equally with men at work, and less than a third of them said they expected women's lives to improve over the next two decades. Yet, only 26% of the women said they felt a need for a strong and organized women's movement. In a similar survey of American women, a much smaller 29% believed they were treated unfairly at work, most were optimistic about the future for women, and 37% said a women's movement was needed.

Japanese companies dramatically increased their hiring of college-educated women in professional jobs after Japan's Diet, or parliament, passed a law barring sex discrimination in the workplace in 1986. The government's aims were to alleviate a growing labor shortage and bolster Japan's image abroad—not to meet demands from Japanese women.

Unlike in the U.S., where women have aggressively fought for equality, women here have hardly raised a whimper. Much to the government's dismay, many professional women are indifferent toward a long-term career.

Early Bow-Outs

Women make up 40% of Japan's work force, including part-timers, but only 1% of them hold managerial positions. And labor specialists estimate that between 25% and 60% of the women who began corporate careers here four years ago have already quit their jobs. According to a 1989 survey by Labor Administration Inc., a government-affiliated research concern, the attrition rate for professional men was just 11% four years after the start of their careers. The same survey found the attrition rate for all female college graduates at Japanese companies, including those traditional clerical jobs, was 45%.

"I intended to stop working when I had my child," says 28-year-old Sayuki Kanda, who left her Tokyo-based textile company last year after working as a public relations officer for five years. Although she enjoyed her responsibility, Ms. Kanda says she can't be persuaded to return to the corporate ladder. "In the end, large companies are a male-oriented society. It's not a place for women to work for life." After having three children, Ms. Kanda plans to do some part-time work.

But many companies realize that with the increasing labor shortage, somehow they'll have to think of a way to attract more women and encourage them to stay. Sumitomo Bank is hiring 250 women out of college this spring, out of 864 new hires, on a "new career track." Asahi breweries recently hired 110 women out of its 900 new marketers, and has started sending them to sell Asahi products to liquor stores—long considered a man's domain.

Greener Pastures

Not all of the women who abandon corporate careers return to hearth and home. Some join small companies or foreign firms that have an image of being more evenhanded. Others enroll in U.S. graduate schools or start their own business.

Those who stay confront a business world still sharply divided by sex. The middle-aged men who run Japanese companies expect professional women to tackle work just like men, in an unflagging manner, described as "bari-bari"—literally, "a crunching sound." And yet they routinely insist on rules for women that they wouldn't dream of imposing on men. (The 1986 law barring sex discrimination established no penalties for violations.) Some require career women in their mid-20s to wear company uniforms, live in company dormitories, and observe a 10 p.m. curfew and get their parent's consent before taking assignments abroad.

A few stodgy banks have a "custom" for a woman—professional or clerical—to quit if she marries someone within the company. The reasoning for this, the banks say, is that if a husband is transferred, as is common every few years, it would be too difficult to also transfer the wife.

Sumitomo Banks insists that women in professional jobs initially wear the same navy blue corporate uniform worn by its secretaries, known as "office ladies" or "OLs." It says this makes less blatant the labeling of career and non-career women, which might upset the OLs.

No one complains. Kazumi Tamai, who was hired for Sumitomo's corporate research department four years ago, says she accepted the uniform because she didn't want customers to ask why she was the only woman wearing regular clothes. "It's not something to raise your voice about," she says. After two years, professional women may wear their own clothes.

Many confess they aren't as committed as their male colleagues to the life of a careerist in a Japanese company, which typically requires late hours, after-work drinking sessions with colleagues and a pledge of allegiance to the company until retirement. By comparison, the image of a housewife, who is free to go shopping, play tennis and perhaps hold a side job or two, is more attractive to many women. "Japanese men are such workaholics," says Ochanomizu's Ms. Shinotsuka. "The women have doubts about having to work like the men."

They also seem to share Japanese society's assumptions that men and women have different roles. Most agree that when a woman marries, taking care of her husband and children should be her priority.

For now, Ms. Tamai is throwing herself into her career. She eats lunch with the men's group and drinks with them after work. She says her dream is to continue the life of a "salaryman."

B. Discussing Information and Issues Presented in the Reading

1. Using what you know from the article on the women's movement in Japan and from the lecture on the women's movement in the United States, compare and contrast the situation of a typical married woman with professional training in Japan with the situation of a typical married woman with professional training in the United States. What aspects of the American system might seem undesirable to a Japanese woman? How might an American woman feel about having to work within the Japanese system?

2. Describe the situation of professional women in your own country. Consider these aspects of the roles professional women play: (1) the number of women who work outside the home; (2) the types of occupations that are commonly open to women; (3) the amount of housework men are willing to help with; (4) the amount of

money women receive when compared to the amount men receive for performing the same job.

3. Is there a women's movement in your country? Is such a movement needed? Explain why or why not. If there is a movement, describe the current women's movement in your country, and if you think a woman's movement is necessary, describe the type of movement that you think would be ideal.

4. The article states that many people in Japanese society agree, "that men and women have different roles. Most agree that when a woman marries, taking care of her husband and children should be her priority." Do you personally agree or disagree with this statement? Be sure to give reasons and examples to support your opinion.

Journal Writing

Respond to the following question in your journal: Should men help with the housework and the raising of children? Explain why they should or should not. Is it acceptable for a husband to take over all duties in the house if his wife has a full-time job that pays a salary sufficient to support the family? Why or why not?

Research Project

Individually or in a group, research one of the following topics and prepare an oral presentation (or a paper) on the information learned about the topic. You may wish to use the Internet, as well as books, to locate interesting information.

    a. Women's health issues including (but not limited to) the eating disorders anorexia and bulimia

    b. Domestic violence: its cause and prevention

    c. Salary comparison for women and men in ＿＿＿＿＿＿＿ (name country/region)

    d. Famous women of ＿＿＿＿＿＿＿ (name of country/region)

    e. Infamous women of ＿＿＿＿＿＿＿ (name of country/region)

    f. Political issues of importance to women in ＿＿＿＿＿＿＿ (name of country/region)

    g. Social issues of importance to women in ＿＿＿＿＿＿＿ (name of country/region)

    h. Sexual harassment in the workplace and in public

The Men's Movement:
What Does It Mean to Be a Man?

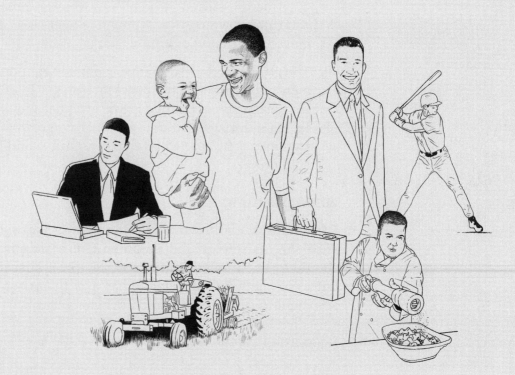

THINK ABOUT AND DISCUSS THE MEANING OF THE FOLLOWING QUOTATION:

Men are men before they are lawyers, or physicians, or merchants, or manufacturers; and if you make them capable and sensible men, they will make themselves capable and sensible lawyers or physicians.

—John Stuart Mill (1806–1873)

English philosopher and economist

a. A man invites a woman to lunch and she declines.

b. A man invites a male friend to lunch and he declines.

c. A woman needs her husband to help with something at home.

d. A man needs his wife to help with something at home.

e. A student asks a professor for an extra day to complete an assignment that is due.

4. What are some politeness strategies that exist in your native language? Are these strategies similar to or different from politeness strategies in English? Describe these differences to the class and relate any miscommunication that you think could occur between people from the U.S. and your culture.

Journal Writing

Respond to the following in your journal: Interview five Americans to find out if they believe American men and women have different ways of expressing themselves, and how these styles of communication differ. Also, ask the interviewee if he or she can share any proverbs about these different styles, like the one you heard in the lecture about foxes' tails and women's tongues. Report your findings in your journal.

Research Project

Find six informants who are not in your class: three men and three women. Show the two photographs on page 98 to each informant. Proceed as follows:

1. Interview each informant individually.

2. Tell your informants to study each picture carefully for a few minutes.

3. Ask your informants to describe each picture carefully.

4. Instruct them to use as many adjectives as they can to clearly describe the picture, including the action, clothing, facial expressions, and so forth.

5. Record or transcribe your informants' responses as accurately as you can.

6. Compare the adjectives and expressions used by the male informants with those used by the female informants. Note the similarities and differences of the language used by each of the subjects.

7. Prepare a report for the class summarizing your findings.

Unit Four	**Communication:**
	The Influence of Language, Culture, and Gender

Part One: Short-Answer Questions

Answer each question by referring to the notes that you took while listening to the lectures in this unit.

Chapter 7   Classroom Communication: Language and Culture in the Classroom

1. Define the term *communication*.

2. What is the title of the article by Andersen and Powell on which this lecture is based?

3. Define *ritual* and give one example of a classroom ritual.

4. Which group of students mentioned in the lecture generally believe that they will learn best by listening to and absorbing the knowledge being given to them by the teacher?

5. According to Andersen and Powell, in which country is classroom communication very tightly controlled by the teacher?

6. Which culture mentioned considers teachers to be honored members of society?

7. According to the lecture, students of what nationality value the personal opinions of the instructor and do not customarily disagree with a teacher?

Chapter 8   **Gender and Communication: Male–Female Conversation as Cross-cultural Communication**

1. Define the term *gender*.

2. Who wrote the book *You Just Don't Understand*?

3. List three characteristics of typical boys' play.

4. List three characteristics of typical girls' play.

5. In Marjorie Harnass Goodwin's research, what task did the girls perform?

6. How does the structure of the girls' game "house" differ from the structure of other girls' games like hopscotch and jump rope?

7. What common stereotype about women is disproved by the studies that examined talk by male and female professors in university meetings?

8. Name the culture in which a wife is expected to paraphrase any words that sound like the name of her father-in-law or brothers.

Part Two: Essay Questions

Answer each essay question below in a paragraph. Use the notes that you took on the lectures to provide support for the claims you make in your essay.

1. Explain how people's perceptions of reality and their behavior are shaped by culture. Consider an individual's mental picture of a classroom and the stereotype that women talk more than men when answering.

2. Analyze the ways that children's play can shape the patterns of communication children later adopt when they grow up.

3. Compare and contrast the communication patterns in typical North American boys' games and typical North American girls' games.

4. Name two aspects of communication that are affected by culture and provide specific examples of how these aspects of communication differ among cultures.

5. Agree or disagree with the following statement: "Male–female conversation is not cross-cultural communication." Be sure to support your argument with facts and details.

6. Define cross-cultural communication using examples from the two lectures.

Part Three: Constructing Test Questions

Use the notes that you took on the lectures in Unit Four to write three test questions about each lecture. After you write the questions, ask a classmate to use his or her notes to answer the questions.

Biology:
Understanding Genetics to Genetic Engineering

THINK ABOUT AND DISCUSS THE MEANING OF THE FOLLOWING QUOTATION:

Biology once was regarded as a languid, largely descriptive discipline, a passive science that was content, for much of its history, merely to observe the natural world rather than change it. No longer. Today biology, armed with the power of genetics, has replaced physics as the activist Science of the Century and it stands poised to assume godlike powers of creation, calling forth artificial forms of life rather than undiscovered elements and subatomic particles.

—Barry Commoner

Senior scientist at Queen's College, City University of New York. Cited in *Harper's Magazine*, February 2002

After all, a single gram of dried DNA, about the size of a half-inch sugar cube, can hold as much information as a trillion compact discs. Adleman senses that can be exploited somehow, some way. One problem is that setting up DNA computers and extracting results from them can take days or weeks. Perhaps a bigger obstacle is controlling biological developments to generate accurate calculations. DNA doesn't always behave like it's expected to.

Columbia University researcher Milan Strojanovic is developing a biology-based machine that doesn't need human help to compute.

Ehud Shapiro of Israel's Weizmann Institute of Science envisions programming molecules with medical information and injecting them into people. He received a U.S. patent in 2001 for a "computer" within a single droplet of water that uses DNA molecules and enzymes as input, output, software and hardware.

Reprinted with permission of The Associated Press.

D. Discussing Information and Issues Presented in the Reading

1. What fueled Leonard Adleman's belief that human cells and computers process and store information in "much the same way"?

2. Describe the similarities and differences in the ways computers and humans store information.

3. Describe the biology-based computers that are being created by scientists and explain the following: (1) what they can do in the year 2003; and (2) what scientists hope they will be able to do in the future. Give examples to support each of your responses.

4. What classic problem did Adleman use his DNA computer to solve? Explain the solution of the problem.

5. What realization has "tempered initial expectations that DNA would ultimately replace silicon chips"? What does this realization have to do with computer chips?

6. The use of DNA computation may have implications for what field? Provide an example.

Journal Writing

Respond to one of the following in your journal.

1. Genetic engineering is a test tube science and is prematurely applied in food production. Agree or disagree and explain why you feel this way.

2. Jeremy Rifkin, author of *The Biotech Century*, claims that our way of life is likely to be more fundamentally transformed in the next several decades than in the previous one thousand years. What is your sense of the accuracy or inaccuracy of Rifkin's claim?

3. Animal and human cloning could become commonplace in the coming decades, with "replication" partially replacing "reproduction" for the first time in history. What will be the ramifications

for people, or for animals, if, indeed, replication replaces reproduction? Are you in favor of (or against) the idea?

4. Some couples (young and old) might choose, in the future, to have their children conceived in test tubes and gestated in artificial wombs to ensure a safe and transparent environment through which to monitor their unborn child's development. Is this a good idea or not? Why?

5. For those who believe technology has made our life worse, James Martin, author of *The Wired Society* (published in 1977), comments, "We have now put ourselves in a position where, if we wanted to return to nature, nature could feed only about 500 million people on Earth. Without technology, we could not feed the 6 billion we are feeding now [in 1977], much less than the 9 billion who will be living on this planet by 2050." Will technology be needed to help feed the people of Earth almost 50 years from now? Explain why or why not.

Research Project

Individually or in a group, research one of the following topics. Write a short paper on the topic, or plan and present a group presentation to inform the class about the topic.

1. One drop of blood has enough DNA to use gene technology to determine a person's DNA profile. Thanks to gene technology, many criminal cases have been solved and many paternity disputes have been settled. Research this topic further on the Internet or in a biology textbook to find out how criminal cases or paternity suits can be settled with genetic testing of an ounce of blood.

2. Research the types of food available that are commonly genetically engineered. List the foods that are eaten by the general public. Ask people in your community if they are aware that these foods are genetically engineered.

INFORMATION RECALL TEST

Unit Five | **Biology:**
Understanding Genetics to Genetic Engineering

Part One: Short-Answer Questions

Answer each question by referring to the notes you took while listening to the lectures in this unit.

Chapter 9 **The Origins of Genetics: Mendel and the Garden Pea**

1. What is the function of genes in people and animals?

2. Where are genes found in the body and how are they transmitted through the generations?

3. Provide at least three examples of inherited traits.

4. Provide an example to support the idea that "humans share many of the same genes with other kinds of animals."

5. Define the terms *genetics* and *geneticists*.

6. Specify the following:
   a. the dates of Mendel's life
   b. the dates Mendel experimented and kept record on 28,000 pea plants

7. To what were the Mendelian Laws of Heredity related.

8. Explain when Mendel studied mathematics at the University of Vienna, and why he did not complete his studies.

9. Explain why the lecturer used the example of racehorses in the lecture, and name the racehorses mentioned by the lecturer.

10. The lecturer mentioned another early pioneer in the study of heredity and genetics whose work Mendel decided to repeat. Who was this pioneer and what did he do?

11. Explain why Mendel used a plant rather than an animal on which to do his heredity experiments.

12. Explain what was so amazing about Mendel's record keeping of his work on the 28,000 plants.

Chapter 10   Genetic Engineering in the Biotech Century: Playing It Smart or Playing Roulette with Mother Nature's Designs?

1. How did the lecturer distinguish between what he talked about in the previous lecture? In other words, how did he establish the continuity of the topic of the second lecture with the first?

2. State the topics about genetic engineering the lecturer dealt with in lecture 2.

3. Define the following terms:
   a. Vesicles
   b. Super animals
   c. Transgenic animals
   d. Animal organ donors

4. Name a number of diseases that are thought to be inherited from parents, relatives, or long-ago ancestors.

5. State what hospitals are requiring for newborn babies in the United States after the year 2004.

6. The famous Dolly has sparked a controversy in science and ethics. What is that controversy?

7. Indicate the two main purposes for which biologists are using genetic engineering.

8. Provide an example of (1) the potential benefits, and (2) the potential dangers of the genetic engineering of crops.

9. How is genetic engineering being used by pharmaceutical companies around the world?

Answer each essay question below in a paragraph. Use the notes you took on the lectures to support the claims you make in your essay.

1. Explain at least three functions of genes in people, animals, insects, and plants, and describe an experiment that could be carried out (other than the one done by Mendel) to study how a trait or characteristic is passed from one generation to another. Be creative, if not totally scientific, in your description.

2. Make some assumptions about Gregor Mendel's personality and intelligence based on his time at the University of Vienna, and his studies of the pea plant.

3. Explain why people are interested in "breeding" insects, plants, animals, and even humans. Give specific examples of why people would want to know how to control each of these species.

4. Explain how Mendel built on the work of the genetics pioneer named Knight. Think of another early pioneer of medicine, biology, chemistry, ecology (or another field) whose work laid the foundation of discoveries in science that contributed to the advance of science or technology. Name the person and describe his or her contribution to science or technology.

5. Agree or disagree with the statement: Humans should continue to seek ways to selectively breed insects, plants, and animals, and people for the betterment of humankind. Give specific reasons for or against this notion.

6. Synthesize the **controversial** issues (both general and personal) involving the use of genetic engineering in medicine and agriculture.

7. Explain (1) the purpose of the genetically engineering microorganism *klebsiella planticola*, (2) the danger the microorganism posed, and (3) the way in which the danger of *klebsiella planticola* was reduced.

8. Agree or disagree with the statement "I am in favor of pursuing research and development of genetic engineering in agriculture and/or medicine." Support your opinion with statements used by the lecturer, as well as other factual or personal-opinion statements. Be sure to indicate the following: (1) statements (or paraphrases) the lecturer used; (2) additional factual examples; and (3) your own personal-opinion examples.

Part Three: Constructing Test Questions

Use the notes you took on the lecture in Unit Five to write three test questions about each lecture. After you write the questions, ask a classmate to use his or her notes to answer the questions.

APPENDIX A: AUDIOSCRIPTS

<table>
<tr><td>Unit One</td><td>

Anthropology:
The Evolution of Human Endeavor

</td></tr>
</table>

Chapter 1   Anthropology: The Study of Human Beings and Their Creations

🎧 A. Orientation Listening Script

The Greek word for "man" is "anthropos" and the word *anthropology* has been in the English language for centuries. But just what does the word mean? Literally anthropology means "the study of man." However, as British philosopher Alfred North Whitehead noted, "It is a well-founded historical generalization that the last thing to be discovered in any science is what the science is really about." And as Paul Bohannan, renowned anthropologist, pointed out a number of years ago, "Each science that deals with people has its own definitions of *human*. An Economist," he explains, "defines a human as a choice-making animal. Philosophers define man as a rationalizing animal. . . ." Anthropology attempts to be all-inclusive—the study of human behavior in all places and throughout time. It specializes in the description of humanistic, scientific, biological, historical, psychological, and social views of humans.

To paraphrase Barbara Miller's statement in her textbook, *Cultural Anthropology*, the popular impression of anthropology is based mainly on movies and television shows that depict anthropologists as adventurers and heroes. Some do have adventures and discover treasures in Egyptian tombs and elsewhere, but mostly, their work is less glamorous and involves repetitive and tedious activities. Until around the middle of the nineteenth century, *anthropology* was a term used for all humanists. My lecture today explains the fields and branches of anthropology. We're going to begin by stating that anthropology is the study of human behavior in all places and at all times.

Western civilization takes credit for the development of anthropology, which, as a matter of fact, was a relatively late science. Earlier Greek and Roman philosophers were more interested in speculating about the ideal society rather than describing those known to them.

After the onset of the Age of Exploration, which included the discovery of the Americas, as well as travel to other distant places, the study of non-Western people began in earnest. In modern day, anthropology is a recognized social science with two broad fields and several branches or subfields.

The two broad fields are physical anthropology and cultural anthropology. Let me give you a brief description of each. Physical anthropology is concerned with the development of man as a mammal. Related subjects are anatomy, biology, and paleontology. Physical anthropologists study the evolution of the human species. One way they do this is by the comparative analysis of fossils—preserved remnants of once-living creatures and living primates, which include human beings or *Homo sapiens.* Common fossils are shells, bones, and molds or imprints. These are found buried in the earth or permanently frozen in glaciers. Living primates are analyzed in order to study the mechanics of evolution and genetic differences among human populations.

Next let's talk about cultural anthropology. This field is the study of learned behavior in human societies. Most cultural anthropologists limit themselves to a few geographic areas, for example, Margaret Mead in Samoa and New Guinea, and Clyde Kluckhohn with the Navajo Indians in the Southwestern United States. I should mention that Kluckhohn's work *Mirror for Man* is considered one of the best introductions to anthropology. Cultural anthropology and the scientific study of human culture will be discussed in more detail in our next lecture. The subfields of cultural anthropology are archaeology, linguistics, and ethnography.

Archaeology is the study of different cultures through material sources rather than direct interviews or observations of the group under study. One example of a famous archaeological site discovered in the past century was King Tut's Tomb near Luxor, Egypt, in 1922.

Linguistics, as you probably know, is the study of language as communication among humans. Culture is learned and transmitted primarily through language.

Ethnography is the systematic description of human societies, mostly based on firsthand fieldwork. Based on ethnographies, anthropologists provide ethnologies or explanations of the behavior of different peoples. A second subfield of ethnography is social anthropology. Social anthropology is concerned with people as social beings. A related subject is, of course, sociology.

Let me also mention briefly psychological anthropology, which deals with human personality and feelings. These are greatly influenced by an individual's biological and mental characteristics, as well as physical surroundings and personal experiences. Related subjects are psychology and psychiatry.

It is important to note that there are several universals common among all societies; for example, the basic similarities in human biology and the existence of two sexes. Another of these is education—either formal or informal or both. Education is necessary to provide the young with the skills and attitudes needed to carry on as adults.

So, you might ask, what are the practical applications for such a broad field? The answer is that anthropology helps us plan the future and helps us contribute to the solution of human problems. This newest area of the study of man is applied anthropology. Formerly, anthropology was limited to the academic field. Anthropologists were teachers or museum curators. But for the past several decades large numbers of "anthro" graduates have been employed in fields such as urban planning and administration, health care, and international development. Most important is that although anthropologists have taken up the task of documenting the processes and changes of cultures past and present, they also provide the necessary insights into where the human species is heading.

🎧 *B. Listening and Notetaking Script*

The Greek word for "man" is "anthropos" and the word *anthropology* has been in the English language for centuries. But just what does the word mean? Literally anthropology means "the study of man." However, as British philosopher Alfred North Whitehead noted, "It is a well-founded historical generalization that the last thing to be discovered in any science is what the science is really about." And as Paul Bohannan, renowned anthropologist, pointed out a number of years ago, "Each science that deals with people has its own definitions of *human*. An Economist," he explains, "defines a human as a choice-making animal. Philosophers define man as a rationalizing animal. . . ." Anthropology attempts to be all-inclusive—the study of human behavior in all places and throughout time. It specializes in the description of humanistic, scientific, biological, historical, psychological, and social views of humans.

Let's review some of the information you just heard to help you with your notetaking. Check your notes and fill in any information you didn't have time to take down the first time you heard it. If you didn't get a chance to write down all that you wanted to write down, did you at least make some notations so that you could review the notes later and complete the missing information. Let's see. The lecturer began with the Greek word for man. *Did you get the spelling of anthropos? It's a-n-t-h-r-o-p-o-s. So what is the meaning of anthropology? Literally, it is the study of man. What was the name of the British philosopher? Did you get his full name? Alfred North Whitehead. What was his message about science? He said the last thing to be discovered in any science is what it is really about. Is Paul Bohannan a physical or social anthropologist? You're correct if you wrote social. Now let's return to the lecture.*

To paraphrase Barbara Miller's statement in her textbook, *Cultural Anthropology*, the popular impression of anthropology is based mainly on movies and television shows that depict anthropologists as adventurers and heroes. Some do have adventures and discover treasures in Egyptian tombs and elsewhere, but mostly, their work is less glamorous and involves repetitive and tedious activities. Until around the middle of the nineteenth century, *anthropology* was a term used for all **humanists.** My lecture today explains the fields and branches of anthropology. We're going to begin by stating that anthropology is the study of human behavior in all places and at all times.

Western civilization takes credit for the development of anthropology, which, as a matter of fact, was a relatively late science. Earlier Greek and Roman philosophers were more interested in speculating about the ideal society rather than describing those known to them.

What year did Barbara Miller publish Cultural Anthropology? *Was it 1899 or 1999? According to her, what is the impression of anthropology based on? How are anthropologists depicted? Prior to the 1850s what was the term "anthropology" used for? What is the lecturer's definition? Who takes credit for the development of anthropology? What were the ancient philosophers interested in? Is this information in your notes? Now let's continue.*

After the onset of the Age of Exploration, which included the discovery of the Americas, as well as travel to other distant places, the study of non-Western people began in earnest. In modern day, anthropology is a recognized social science with two broad fields and several branches or subfields.

The two broad fields are physical anthropology and cultural anthropology. Let me give you a brief description of each. Physical anthropology is concerned the development of man as a mammal. Related subjects are anatomy, biology, and paleontology. Physical anthropologists study the evolution of the human species. One way they do this is by the comparative analysis of fossils—preserved remnants of once-living creatures and living primates, which include human beings or *Homo sapiens.* Common fossils are shells, bones, and molds or imprints. These are found buried in the earth or permanently frozen in glaciers. Living primates are analyzed in order to study the mechanics of evolution and genetic differences among human populations.

What was the period of travel and discovery of new places called? Did you write down the phrase: **the Age of Exploration?** *Do you have the descriptions of the two main branches of anthropology? What are the related subjects of physical anthropology? What are fossils? Did you take down three kinds that were mentioned? What was another word for molds? Where are fossils found? Check your notes.*

Next let's talk about cultural anthropology. This field is the study of learned behavior in human societies. Most cultural anthropologists limit themselves to a few geographic areas, for example, Margaret Mead in Samoa and New Guinea, and Clyde Kluckhohn with the Navajo Indians in the Southwestern United States. I should mention that Kluckhohn's work *Mirror for Man* is considered one of the best introductions to anthropology. Cultural anthropology and the scientific study of human culture will be discussed in more detail in our next lecture. The subfields of cultural anthropology are archaeology, linguistics, and ethnography.

Archaeology is the study of different cultures through material sources rather than direct interviews or observations of the group under study. One example of a famous archaeological site discovered in the past century was King Tut's Tomb near Luxor, Egypt, in 1922.

Linguistics, as you probably know, is the study of language as communication among humans. Culture is learned and transmitted primarily through language.

Ethnography is the systematic description of human societies, mostly based on firsthand fieldwork. Based on ethnographies, anthropologists provide ethnologies or explanations of the behavior of different peoples. A second subfield of ethnography is social anthropology. Social anthropology is concerned with people as social beings. A related subject is, of course, sociology.

Let me also mention briefly psychological anthropology, which deals with human personality and feelings. These are greatly influenced by an individual's biological and mental characteristics, as well as physical surroundings and personal experiences. Related subjects are psychology and psychiatry.

There were a lot of details in this part of the lecture. Let's backtrack a bit. Let me spell the last names of the two anthropologists just mentioned. Margaret Mead—that's M-e-a-d—and Clyde Kluckhohn—K-l-u-c-k-h-o-h-n. Did you write down the three subfields of cultural anthropology that the speaker mentioned? They were archaeology, linguistics, and ethnography. To save time, you can check the spelling later. Note the mention of psychological anthropology. What is it concerned with? What are the related subjects? Now let's see what the speaker talks about next.

It is important to note that there are several universals common among all societies, for example, the basic similarities in human biology and the existence of two sexes. Another of these is education—either formal or informal or both. Education is necessary to provide the young with the skills and attitudes needed to carry on as adults.

So, you might ask, what are the practical applications for such a broad field? The answer is that anthropology helps us plan the future and helps us contribute to the solution of human problems. This newest area of the study of man is applied anthropology. Formerly, anthropology was limited to the academic field. Anthropologists were teachers or museum curators. But for the past several decades large numbers of "anthro" graduates have been employed in fields such as urban planning and administration, health care, and international development. Most important is that although anthropologists have taken up the task of documenting the processes and changes of cultures past and present, they also provide the necessary insights into where the human species is heading.

What were the universals mentioned? What are the practical applications of the field? Where did we mostly find cultural anthropologists in the past? Did you take down all the job areas mentioned? What were they? Right—urban planning, health care, and international development. Finally, according to the lecturer, what valuable insight does the anthropologist provide?

Unit One | **Anthropology:**
The Evolution of Human Endeavor

Chapter 2   The Concept of Culture: Understanding One Another

A. Orientation Listening Script

Let me begin the lecture today by asking, "What exactly is culture?" This question has been approached by anthropologists in many different ways. Murdock, for example, in *Outline of World Cultures,* produced what many have called the ultimate laundry list of things cultural by naming 900-odd categories of human behavior. I won't attempt to go into these at this time. Another less lengthy list is the famous "grocery list" of Edward B. Tyler. He wrote, "Culture is that complex whole which includes knowledge, belief, art, morals, custom, and any other capabilities and habits acquired by man as a member of society." But another definition of culture that many find useful is, "the totality of learned, socially transmitted behavior." Obviously this definition leaves out much if we feel obligated to include all the ways of life that have been evolved by people in every society.

A particular culture, then, would mean the total shared way of life of a given group. This would include their ways of thinking, acting, and feeling as reflected in their religion, law, language, art, and customs, as well as concrete things such as houses, clothing, and tools. Cultural anthropology is the study of cultures—living and dead. In its totality, it includes linguistics, the study of speech forms, archaeology (the study of dead cultures), and ethnology, which is the study of living cultures or those that can be observed directly.

Why study cultural anthropology? One reason noted by Ruth Benedict, another well-known anthropologist, is that the story of humanity from the Stone Age to the present is such a fascinating one of cultural growth. Interestingly, every society has gone through three stages or steps of cultural growth. These are savagery, barbarism, and finally, civilization. The last is, of course, to varying degrees.

We are often reminded of another compelling reason to learn about different cultures—to learn and use a foreign language effectively. Most of us realize that just knowing the language of another culture is not enough for meaningful communication. You can ask anyone who has tried to use their high school Spanish inside a Spanish-speaking country.

Ned Seelye, in his 1993 book *Teaching Culture*, lists six skills to nurture and support intercultural communication:

Number 1: Cultivate curiosity about another culture and empathy toward its members.

Number 2: Recognize that different roles and other social variables such as age, sex, social class, religion, ethnicity, and place of residence affect the way people speak and behave.

Number 3: Realize that effective communication requires discovering the culturally conditioned images of people when they think, act, and react to the world around them.

Number 4: Recognize that situational variables and conventions shape people's behavior in important ways.

Number 5: Understand that people generally act the way they do because they are exercising the options their society allows for satisfying basic physical and psychological needs.

And, finally, number 6: Develop the ability to evaluate the truth of a generalization about the target culture and to locate and organize information about the target culture from books, mass media, people, and personal observations.

Culture and society must coexist. Without living together people cannot create a culture or way of life. If a group or society is small, isolated, and stable, it might also share a single culture. For example, think of the Tasaday, allegedly a Stone Age people in the Philippine rain forest, who were discovered by anthropologists back in 1971. A side note is that due to their supposed isolation, they had no weapons or known words in their language for "enemy" or "war." In your reading after the lecture, you'll learn more about the Tasaday and the controversy surrounding them up to the present time.

It is important to remember, however, that large societies, such as those in Canada, the United States, India, or Egypt, are multicultural or "pluralist" societies. They also tend to have many subcultures. In the long history of human life, multiculturalism is a fairly recent phenomenon. Those of us in multicultural environments must remember that discovering similarities among people from different cultures is as important as identifying differences. For example, in classrooms on just about every university campus in the world, we find students from many different social and ethnic backgrounds. What are some of the "universals" that you and other international students have all experienced in your earlier educational life?

One common universal is that all cultures use rewards and punishments to encourage correct behavior. Another example is that societies withhold certain information from the young. This might include faults in our leaders or sexual taboos. A third universal is the effort by the controlling group in a culture to educate the young to strengthen and secure its dominant position. In the majority of contemporary societies this control is reached through political means in contrast to the military actions of earlier times, such as the Roman Conquests and the Moorish invasions.

In closing this lecture on societies and culture, let me remind you not to forget the contributions of thoughts and actions of the individual person in a group. Note the observation of Edward Sapir, another famous anthropologist: "It is always the individual that really thinks and acts and dreams and revolts." Obviously the concept of culture will be argued by anthropologists for years to come.

Chapter 2   The Concept of Culture: Understanding One Another

⌯ B. Listening and Notetaking Script

Let me begin the lecture today by asking, "What exactly is culture?" This question has been approached by anthropologists in many different ways. Murdock, for example, in *Outline of World Cultures*, produced what many have called the ultimate laundry list of things cultural by naming 900-odd categories of human behavior. I won't attempt to go into these at this time. But another less lengthy list is the famous "grocery list" of Edward B. Tyler. He wrote, "Culture is that complex whole which includes knowledge, belief, art, morals, custom, and any other capabilities and habits acquired by man as a member of society." Another definition of culture that many find useful is, "the totality of learned, socially transmitted behavior." Obviously this definition leaves out much if we feel obligated to include all the ways of life that have been evolved by people in every society.

The lecturer has given us a lot of information and a lot to think about in these opening lines. How many categories did George P. Murdock name in his book? Did you get the name of the book? It was Outline of World Cultures. *What did she call Tyler's definition of culture?*

A particular culture, then, would mean the total shared way of life of a given group. This would include their ways of thinking, acting, and feeling as reflected in their religion, law, language, art, and customs, as well as concrete things such as houses, clothing, and tools. Cultural anthropology is the study of cultures—living and dead. In its totality, it includes linguistics, the study of speech forms, archaeology (the study of dead cultures), and ethnology, which is the study of living cultures or those than can be observed directly.

Why study cultural anthropology? One reason noted by Ruth Benedict, another well-known anthropologist, is that the story of humanity from the Stone Age to the present is such a fascinating one of cultural growth. Interestingly, every society has gone through three stages or steps of cultural growth. These are savagery, barbarism, and finally, civilization. The last is, of course, to varying degrees.

We are often reminded of another compelling reason to learn about different cultures—to learn and use a foreign language effectively. Most of us realize that just knowing the language of another culture is not enough for meaningful communication. You can ask anyone who has tried to use their high school Spanish inside a Spanish-speaking country.

Did you get the three steps of cultural growth or development? They are savagery, barbarism, and civilization. Savagery is a form of primitive behavior; barbarism refers to an uncivilized condition. To the Greeks and Romans, it was a term for foreigners. Civilization is social organization with government and cultural complexity. The learning of a foreign language was mentioned next. Did you jot down the phrase, "meaningful communication"?

Ned Seelye, in his 1993 book *Teaching Culture*, lists six skills to nurture and support intercultural communication:

Number 1: Cultivate curiosity about another culture and empathy toward its members.

Remember to use abbreviations to keep up with the lecturer. For example culture can be shortened to cult. That's c-u-l-t period. As the lecture continues you should get better at developing your own system. It's important, however, that you have no problem understanding your abbreviations.

Number 2: Recognize that different roles and other social variables such as age, sex, social class, religion, ethnicity, and place of residence affect the way people speak and behave.

Number 3: Realize that effective communication requires discovering the culturally conditioned images of people when they think, act, and react to the world around them.

Number 4: Recognize that situational variables and conventions shape people's behavior in important ways.

Number 5: Understand that people generally act the way they do because they are exercising the options their society allows for satisfying basic physical and psychological needs.

And, finally, number 6: Develop the ability to evaluate the truth of a generalization about the target culture and to locate and organize information about the target culture from books, mass media, people, and personal observations.

In writing down the six points in your notes did you use abbreviations and omit many of the unnecessary structure words such as the articles the, a or an? In the first rule did you write down the key words: curiosity, empathy, other cultures. Let me summarize the others:

Rule 2: Recognize different roles and behavior determined by sex, age, social class, religion, ethnicity, place of residence.

Rule 3: Effective communication requires knowing how to recognize how and why people think, act, and react to the world around them.

Rule 4: Situation variables and conventions or customs shape people's behavior in important ways.

Rule 5: People in different societies act they way they do because of the options their society offers them.

And Rule 6: We must learn to get at the truth about the target culture we are trying to understand. Books, mass media, people, and personal observation are all used in this process.

Let's continue with the lecture.

Culture and society must coexist. Without living together people cannot create a culture or way of life. If a group or society is small, isolated, and stable, it might also share a single culture. For example, think of the Tasaday, allegedly a Stone Age people in the Philippine rain forest, who were discovered by anthropologists back in 1971. A side note is that due to their supposed isolation, they had no weapons or known words in their language for "enemy" or "war." In your reading after the lecture, you'll learn more about the Tasaday and the controversy surrounding them up to the present time.

What did the lecturer say is necessary for a group or society to have one culture? She mentioned they must be small, isolated, and stable. In what year were the Tasaday people discovered in the Philippines? Right, it was in 1971. The lecturer said they had no weapons or words for enemy or war. Let's be sure to spell Tasaday correctly: It's T-a-s-a-d-a-y. Let's hear more of the lecture.

It is important to remember, however, that large societies such as those in Canada, the United States, India, or Egypt, are multicultural or "pluralist" societies. They also tend to have many subcultures. In the long history of human life, multiculturalism is a fairly recent phenomenon. Those of us in multicultural environments must remember that discovering similarities among people from different cultures is as important as identifying differences. For example, in classrooms on just about every university campus in the world, we find students from many different social and ethnic backgrounds. What are some of the "universals" that you and other international students have all experienced in your earlier educational life?

One common universal is that all cultures use rewards and punishments to encourage correct behavior. Another example is that societies withhold certain information from the young. This might include faults in our leaders or sexual taboos. A third universal is the effort by the controlling group in a culture to educate the young to strengthen and secure its dominant position. In the majority of contemporary societies this control is reached through political means in contrast to the military actions of earlier times, such as the Roman Conquests and the Moorish invasions.

The last topic was multicultural or pluralistic societies. There were several countries given as examples. Did you write them down? They were Canada, the United States, India, and Egypt.

Did you abbreviate the names? But after mentioning multiculturalism the lecturer discussed universals—in other words, things that are common to different people all over the world. What were the three examples? First, she said we all use rewards and punishments to encourage correct behavior. The second universal was that we hold back certain information from our young people. Let's repeat the examples. They include weaknesses or faults in our political leaders and sexual taboos. The third was that the people in power or in control use education to strengthen and secure their own security and position. Now let's hear the rest of the lecture.

In closing this lecture on societies and culture, let me remind you not to forget the contributions of thoughts and actions of the individual person in a group. Note the observation of Edward Sapir, another famous anthropologist: "It is always the individual that really thinks and acts and dreams and revolts." Obviously the concept of culture will be argued by anthropologists for years to come.

Let me repeat the words of Edward Sapir—that's S-a-p-i-r: He said, "It is always the individual that really thinks and acts and

women are becoming too independent and powerful today as a result of the professional advances they have made in the workplace and because of the personal freedoms they have gained in their family and personal relationships. She notes that the resentment of some men toward women's gaining power is not a recent phenomenon. More than 1,900 years ago, the women of Rome tried to repeal a law that forbade them from riding in horse-drawn chariots and from wearing multicolored dresses. In 195 B.C., the Roman senator Cato expressed the fear and concern that the women of Rome had become so powerful that the independence of the men of Rome had been lost in their homes, and was being trampled underfoot in public. In her recent book titled *Backlash: The Undeclared War Against American Women*, Susan Faludi points out that many men today still resent women's progress in becoming independent personally and professionally. Faludi notes that a seven-year survey of American male attitudes in the 1980s found that no more than 5 to 10 percent of the men surveyed genuinely supported women's demands for independence and equality. It is likely that this attitude has not changed much today.

Although some women view the men's movement as a backlash, many others see the men's movement as something that is good for both men and women. They see it as men's need to form a brotherhood for psychological support to protect their rights and personal freedoms even as women formed support groups with other women to protect and advance their rights. They think, for example, that women should not automatically be given custody of children when a divorce occurs, and yet this is what often happens in the United States today. Finally, some authorities relate the development of the men's movement to the confusion created by the crisis of masculinity in contemporary society, and the many and changing images portrayed in the popular media of who and what real men are and how they are supposed to act. If you watch American movies, you might find yourself asking: Is the real man, for example, a sensitive guy like Dustin Hoffman's *Tootsie*? Is he an involved dad like Robin Williams's *Mrs. Doubtfire* or the father played by Steve Martin in *Parenthood*? A macho man like Arnold Schwarzenegger plays in *The Terminator*, or is he a caring nurturer like the man Schwarzenegger played in *Kindergarten Cop*? Many men are searching for answers to this question and are attempting to find answers from the leaders of the men's movement.

The lecturer started off by listing some of the catalysts for the men's movement and why women view the movement as a reaction against the women's movement. Some men feel that women are too independent and powerful today as a result of professional advances they have made and the personal freedoms they have won. Resentment against women is not new, the speaker said. In ancient Rome, for example, more than 1,900 years ago, women were forbidden from riding in horse-drawn chariots and from wearing multicolored dresses, and they tried to have these laws repealed. The author Susan Faludi, in her book titled Backlash: The Undeclared War Against American Women, *believes that many men today resent women's personal and professional independence. She claims in her book that no more than 5 to 10 percent of the men surveyed genuinely support women's demands for independence and equality.*

At this point, the lecturer changes from talking about the phenomenon of backlash to describing (1) how the movement functions as psychological support for men equivalent to the support women have received from the women's movement, and (2) how the movement helps men cope with the confusion created by the changing images of men in popular movies, like Mrs. Doubtfire, The Terminator, *and* Kindergarten Cop. *Did you write down the types of movies these are? Let's now finish the lecture. You will take notes without any assistance given for this next and final segment of the lecture. Ready?*

What are the origins of this crisis of masculinity that poses problems for many men today? One of the historical reasons for the crisis, according to Robert Bly, a poet who is considered to be one of the founding fathers of the men's movement, is rooted in the changes that took place in the U.S. as a result of the Industrial Revolution, which occurred in the early to mid-1900s. When the Industrial Revolution began, the kinds of work that people did (that is, the kinds of work men did) changed for many Americans. Before the Civil War, 88 percent of American males were small farmers, independent artisans, or small-business owners. In these professions the workers usually worked close to their homes. This meant that sons were constantly learning how to work and support themselves and their family by working alongside their fathers. By 1910, however, less then one-third of all men in the United States were self-employed. Sociologist Michael Kimmel points out that even then many men felt that the concept of manhood was being threatened (and was even vanishing) because men no longer worked their land, or had control over their labor. Many never got to see the fruits of their labor, as farmers and craftsmen usually do. Many men in the post-Industrial Revolution era had become mere cogs in the machines of industrial America. In addition, the change from a farm to an industrial society meant that instead of supporting their families by working near their homes as farmers, craftsmen, or small-business owners, the majority of men began working in factories or offices. Often the factories were far from their homes and men had to travel long distances to work. This meant that the men were not home and the amount of time fathers spent with their sons was greatly reduced. Young boys, therefore, did not have their fathers around to act as role models. The effects of the Industrial Revolution continue into the present day, according to men in the men's movement, and they want to address the problems it has brought. For example, many people are concerned that men still have little say in the upbringing of their children.

The evolution of the women's movement had a profound effect on the development of the men's movement. As a result of the women's movement, more women are working outside the home, and many men are playing a more active role in family life and they are taking on some of the tasks involved in child care and housework. Thirty to forty years ago, care of the home and children were almost exclusively the responsibility of women. In addition to these changes inside the home, in the workplace, men are today entering occupations that used to be considered women's jobs. More men are becoming nurses and teachers of young children. Other men are finding that they have more female colleagues and bosses at work than ever before, and they are having to adapt to women's styles of communication and management, which can differ considerably from those of men. At work, as well as at home, many men today in the U.S. have to play very different roles than their fathers did. As a result, they are joining with other men in the men's movement or they are reading books such as Robert Bly's *Iron John* to try to understand and cope with the roles expected of men in today's world.

So, some of the reasons for the men's movement can be attributed to three things: 1) the changing roles brought about by the women's movement, 2) the Industrial Revolution, and 3) men's desire to understand and affirm the concept of manhood.

Exactly what forms does the men's movement take, and what do men in the men's movement hope to achieve by being active in the movement? To begin with, the men's movement has no unified, monolithic philosophy. Although there are a number of unifying themes, there are also some interesting differences between the basic groups associated with the men's movement. Several writers who write about the men's movement have identified four basic groups of men active in the movement.

The first group is labeled the male feminists, and these men work for women's rights and equality between the sexes. Some of the men in this first group are vocal about blaming other men for much of the violence against women and for the inequality that exists between men and women in relationships and in the job market. Not all members of the men's movement, however, consider this first group of men to be an integral part of the men's movement. To be sure, the other three groups focus more on men's issues than do the so-called male feminists.

The second orientation in the men's movement attracts men who join men's support groups to meet regularly and give and receive psychological support in dealing with problems created by the new roles they have to play at home and at work. These men are attempting to learn to better express their feelings and emotions, and to show sensitivity without being ashamed. A third group in the men's movement consists of men who want to get back the power they feel they have lost because of the advances made by women as a result of the women's movement and feminist causes. Finally, there is an approach to the movement called the mytho-poetic men's movement. The mytho-poetic men's movement is often identified with Robert Bly, the poet who wrote one of the most well-known books of the men's movement: *Iron John*. The men involved in this aspect of the men's movement believe that men should be initiated into manhood as men were initiated when people still lived in small tribes and bands in ancient cultures. This group initiates men using mythology, poetry (hence the name mytho-poetic), and other rituals, such as dancing, to explore and affirm the value of masculinity and masculine approaches to problem solving. Men who subscribe to this viewpoint worry that too much contact with women and too little contact with other men has turned them into weaklings or wimps.

So, the men's movement is very diverse. A man who wants to join the movement has many options of just how he will explore the question "What does it mean to be a man in today's world?"

What do women think of the men's movement? Just as there are many different ways for men to approach the men's movement, there are many different opinions about the value and worth of the movement. Some women, especially many feminists, do not like the men's movement. They feel it is a backlash and that it is an example of how men are trying to keep women from achieving equality by forming stronger "good old boy" (or male-only) networks and by advocating women's return to their roles of housewife and mother rather than business partner or competitor. However, some women, particularly those whose husbands are part of men's support groups or who have gone on men's weekend retreats are glad that men are learning to express their emotions and getting support from other men. Barbara Brotman reports in an article in the *Chicago Tribune* that one woman she interviewed is glad that her husband has joined the men's movement because she no longer feels that she alone is responsible for their family's emotional well-being. She and her husband now share that role and responsibility.

This lecture has been only a brief introduction to some of the issues related to the men's movement. Because of many different perceptions concerning the goals and purpose of the movement, it is difficult to give a simple definition or draw a simple portrait of the movement. Perhaps it would be better to say the men's movement is like a tree with many branches and many roots. The movement is much younger than the women's movement, but in one form or another it is beginning to have substantial impact on many men and women, as they try to adapt to their changing roles in American society in the twenty-first century.

Well, how did you do? Take the time to check your notes with a classmate. Look at your notes and present the information in the final section of the lecture to him or her. Share the task. You present the information in one segment of the lecture, and then allow your classmate to present the information in the next section. If you missed any of the information, you will have an opportunity to complete your notes as you listen to your classmate.

Unit Four | **Communication:**
The Influence of Language, Culture, and Gender

Chapter 7   Classroom Communication: Language and Culture in the Classroom

🎧 A. Orientation Listening Script

Today's lecture deals with the topic of language, culture, and communication in classrooms in the United States. Samovar and Porter, in their book *Intercultural Communication,* define *communication* as a form of human behavior that results from a need to interact with other human beings. As a result of this need, we send verbal and nonverbal messages to communicate with both friends and strangers. Communication can take the form of talk, or it can take the form of gestures, or nonverbal signals, of one kind or another. The talk or signals send messages that communicate a person's thoughts, feelings, and intentions to others. Many scholars study the topic of communication, in general, and speech communication, specifically, in order to learn how individuals send and interpret messages. A number of these scholars conduct research on the topic of intercultural communication. That is, they study communication between people from different cultures. One area of research in intercultural communication is the study of the influence of the setting, or environment, on the success and/or failure of communication. In this lecture, I will be talking about one specific aspect of intercultural communication; that is, intercultural communication that takes place in the classroom. This information is taken from a book chapter written by Janis Andersen and Robert Powell titled "Intercultural Communication and the Classroom." It appeared in Samovar and Porter's edited book *Intercultural Communication.*

When you are asked to picture a classroom in your mind's eye, what do you see? You probably see a classroom that is familiar to you and that would be familiar to students from your culture. However, not everyone will see the same picture in their minds. Although many people have similar images of what a classroom looks like in their mind's eye, their culture greatly influences the way they view the teacher–student relationship, and culture also influences how a person understands the ways in which information is taught and learned in the classroom. Culture also plays an important role in determining how teachers and students communicate in the classroom. In this lecture, I'll give you a few examples of some of the ways that culture affects this communication. The "classroom" as we know it, by the way, is a relatively recent innovation, according to Janis Andersen and Robert Powell. Great teachers like Socrates, Plato, Aristotle, and Confucius taught without the benefit of a board, chalk, desks, and the standard comforts (or discomforts) of a classroom building. But let me return to the main topic of this lecture—the influence of culture on behavior and communication between teacher and students in the classroom.

If you have come from another culture to study in the United States, you may already have noticed that teachers and students in American universities interact and communicate in the classroom in ways that differ from how teachers and students communicate in your home culture. It's culture that influences and establishes these interactions and communication patterns. Of course, culture is a term that is used in many different ways. Basically, culture provides us with a system of knowledge that allows us to communicate with others and teaches us how to interpret their verbal and nonverbal behavior. Culture influences and establishes how people interact with one another (or do not interact with one another). In particular, culture influences the rituals that take place in the classroom setting, and it influences the ways that students participate in the classroom discourse. It also influences the esteem in which teachers are held.

Just what exactly are "rituals"? I'll give you a dictionary definition to begin with. "Rituals" are systematic procedures used to perform a certain act or to communicate a certain message. Well, there are many rituals associated with teaching and learning, and education in general. Rituals are systematic procedures used to perform a certain act or to communicate a certain message. In some countries, when a teacher enters the classroom, the students ritually stand up. In the United States, a classroom ritual occurs when a student raises her hand to signal to the teacher that she knows the answer to a question. This is not a universal classroom ritual to signal intent to answer a question, however. Jamaican students snap or flap their fingers to signal that they want to answer a question that has been posed. In some college- and graduate-level seminars in American universities, students do not make any physical signs when they want to speak; they state their ideas whenever they feel the urge or when it is appropriate. This sort of classroom behavior is especially confusing to students from cultures in which there are no rituals for attracting the teacher's attention because the student is not expected to participate in the class at all.

This brings us to the issue of classroom participation. North American students of European origin are usually more talkative in class and more willing to state their opinions than students of Native American heritage or from Asian backgrounds. This difference is directly related to cultural values about learning and education, and classroom behavior. Euro-American students' culture teaches them that learning is shaped and helped by their talk and active engagement in exploring or discussing issues. Asian students, however, are generally taught that they will learn best by listening to and absorbing the knowledge being given to them by the teacher. In their article, Andersen and Powell point out that some cultures do not have a way for students to signal a desire to talk to a teacher; in these cultures, students speak out only after the teacher has spoken to them. Most classroom interaction in Vietnam is tightly controlled by the teacher, according to Andersen and Powell.

The esteem in which teachers are held also varies from culture to culture. According to researchers Samovar and Porter, the Vietnamese have a great deal of respect for their instructors and consider them to be honored members of society. The Vietnamese and many other Asian peoples see the teacher, the instructor, and the professor as the very "symbol" of learning and culture. In Germany, students value the personal opinions of their instructors and it is not customary to disagree with or contradict a teacher during class. Israeli students, on the other hand, can criticize an instructor if they feel that he or she is wrong about an issue or who they believe has provided incorrect information, according to Samovar and Porter.

There are many other ways that culture can affect interaction and communication between teachers and students in the classroom. I have discussed differences in how students get the teacher's attention during class, and I've pointed out the differences in the ways students from various cultures participate and communicate with the teacher during class. From this brief consideration of classroom communication, you should begin to see that learning a language involves more than studying the vocabulary, idioms, and the grammar of the language. If you are to succeed in communicating in a second-language classroom, you need to learn not only the language spoken in the classroom, but also the expected procedures of classroom participation and communication—that is, the rituals of language, culture, and communication.

Chapter 7   Classroom Communication: Language and Culture in the Classroom

B. Listening and Notetaking Script

Today's lecture deals with the topic of language, culture, and communication in classrooms in the United States. Samovar and Porter, in their book *Intercultural Communication*, define *communication* as a form of human behavior that results from a need to interact with other human beings. As a result of this need, we send verbal and nonverbal messages to communicate with both friends and strangers. Communication can take the form of talk, or it can take the form of gestures, or nonverbal signals, of one kind or another. The talk or signals send messages that communicate a person's thoughts, feelings, and intentions to others. Many scholars study the topic of communication, in general, and speech communication, specifically, in order to learn how individuals send and interpret messages. A number of these scholars conduct research on the topic of intercultural communication. That is, they study communication between people from different cultures. One area of research in intercultural communication is the study of the influence of the setting, or environment, on the success and/or failure of communication. In this lecture, I will be talking about one specific aspect of intercultural communication; that is, intercultural communication that takes place in the classroom. This information is taken from a book chapter written by Janis Andersen and Robert Powell titled "Intercultural Communication and the Classroom." It appeared in Samovar and Porter's edited book *Intercultural Communication*.

When you are asked to picture a classroom in your mind's eye, what do you see? You probably see a classroom that is familiar to you and that would be familiar to students from your culture. However, not everyone will see the same picture in their minds. Although many people have similar images of what a classroom looks like in their mind's eye, their culture greatly influences the way they view the teacher–student relationship, and culture also influences how a person understands the ways in which information is taught and learned in the classroom. Culture also plays an important role in determining how teachers and students communicate in the classroom. In this lecture, I'll give you a few examples of some of the ways that culture affects this communication. The "classroom" as we know it, by the way, is a relatively recent innovation, according to Janis Andersen and Robert Powell. Great teachers like Socrates, Plato, Aristotle, and Confucius taught without the benefit of a board, chalk, desks, and the standard comforts (or discomforts) of a classroom building. But let me return to the main topic of this lecture—the influence of culture on behavior and communication between teacher and students in the classroom.

Let's take a brief break from listening and notetaking to check your notes and give you an opportunity to see how you're doing so far. I'll limit my mentoring to providing an outline of the lecture and asking a few questions that you should be able to answer by looking in your notes.

The speaker opened the lecture with a definition of the term communication. *Check your notes. Can you define the term? You don't have to define it in the exact words the speaker used; you can paraphrase slightly as long as you can provide a definition of the term that captures the meaning given by Samovar and Porter. Did you note their names, even if you didn't get the spelling correct? (pause) OK. The speaker next mentioned why people communicate—they have a need to interact with other human beings—and how they communicate—with verbal and nonverbal messages. Is there anything else you included in your notes about the first few points made by the lecturer? (pause) OK. What did the lecturer discuss next? It involved the research of speech communication scholars and what some of them study. What do some of these speech communication scholars study? Right. Intercultural communication and, more specifically, the influence of the communication setting (for example, the classroom) and the success and/or the failure of the communication. At this point, the lecturer started to get more specific about the kind of intercultural communication he would be dealing with. Check your notes. What was it? I'm confident that you can answer that question. Let me continue. The next topic dealt with was the classroom and culture. The speaker began this section of the lecture asking you to get a picture in your mind's eye of a classroom. Did you note this? Why or why not? What was the point of using the mental-picture technique? You have to decide what you don't need to take down in your notes, and this example was something that could have been omitted, but the important point of why it was used should have found its way into your notes. Can you find the answer to this question in your notes? Let's return to the lecture.*

If you have come from another culture to study in North America, you may already have noticed that teachers and students in American universities interact and communicate in the classroom in ways that differ from how teachers and students communicate in your home culture. It's culture that influences and establishes these interactions and communication patterns. Of course, culture is a term that is used in many different ways. Basically, culture provides us with a system of knowledge that allows us to communicate with others and teaches us how to interpret their verbal and nonverbal behavior. Culture influences and establishes how people interact with one another (or do not interact with one another). In particular, culture influences the rituals that take place in the classroom setting, and it influences the ways that students participate in the classroom discourse. It also influences the esteem in which teachers are held.

Just what exactly are "rituals"? I'll give you a dictionary definition to begin with. "Rituals" are systematic procedures used to perform a certain act or to communicate a certain message. Well, there are many rituals associated with teaching and learning, and education in general. In some countries, when a teacher enters the classroom, the students ritually stand up. In the United States, a classroom ritual occurs when a student raises her hand to signal to the teacher that she knows the answer to a question. This is not a universal classroom ritual to signal intent to answer a question, however. Jamaican students snap or flap their fingers to signal that they want to answer a question that has been posed. In some college- and graduate-level seminars in North American universities, students do not make any physical signs when they want to speak; they state their ideas whenever they feel the urge or when it is appropriate. This sort of classroom behavior is especially confusing to students from cultures in which there are no rituals for attracting the teacher's attention because the student is not expected to participate in the class at all.

This brings us to the issue of classroom participation. North American students of European origin are usually more talkative in class and more willing to state their opinions than students of Native American heritage or from Asian backgrounds. This difference is directly related to cultural values about learning and education, and classroom behavior. Euro-American students' culture teaches them that learning is shaped and helped by their talk and active engagement in exploring or discussing issues. Asian students, however, are generally taught that they will learn best by listening to and absorbing the knowledge being given to them by the teacher. In their article, Andersen and Powell point out that some cultures do not have a way for students to signal a desire to talk to a teacher; in these cultures, students speak out only after the teacher has spoken to them. Most classroom interaction in Vietnam is tightly controlled by the teacher, according to Andersen and Powell.

The esteem in which teachers are held also varies from culture to culture. According to researchers Samovar and Porter, the Vietnamese have a great deal of respect for their instructors and consider them to be honored members of society. The Vietnamese and many other Asian peoples see the teacher, the instructor, and the professor as the very "symbol" of learning and culture. In Germany, students value the personal opinions of their instructors and it is not customary to disagree with or contradict a teacher during class. Israeli students, on the other hand, can criticize an instructor if they feel that he or she is wrong about an issue or who they believe has provided incorrect information, according to Samovar and Porter.

There are many other ways that culture can affect interaction and communication between teachers and students in the classroom. I have discussed differences in how students get the teacher's attention during class, and I've pointed out the differences in the ways students from various cultures participate and communicate with the teacher during class. From this brief consideration of classroom communication, you should begin to see that learning a language involves more than studying the vocabulary, idioms, and the grammar of the language. If you are to succeed in communicating in a second-language classroom, you need to learn not only the language spoken in the classroom, but also the expected procedures of classroom participation and communication— that is, the rituals of language, culture, and communication.

Now, let me mention the main topics of the section of the lecture that you just heard. Check your notes to be sure that you have written down this information.

1. *Classroom rituals—can you define the term* ritual? *Can you give the examples of rituals that were mentioned?*

2. *Classroom participation—can you describe the differences that have been observed between Euro-American and Asian students' participation in class? Are you using your memory or your notes to answer the question? What did the lecturer say about Vietnamese classroom participation patterns?*

3. *The esteem in which teachers are held. Look at your notes and see whether you can summarize the information presented about this topic.*

Finally, what was the last topic dealt with? Did you write it down and can you decode the notes you took to reconstruct the information? If you can, you're making progress in developing your listening comprehension and notetaking skills.

Unit Four | **Communication:**
The Influence of Language, Culture, and Gender

Chapter 8   **Gender and Communication: Male–Female Conversation as Cross-cultural Communication**

In the last lecture, you heard about the relationship between culture and classroom communication. In this lecture, I'll talk about another variable that affects human communication. That variable is gender. Gender is the social identity that men and women learn as they grow up in a culture. For example, boys learn to be "masculine" and girls learn to be "feminine" as they grow to be men and women. Researchers have shown that men and women (and boys and girls, for that matter) communicate in quite different ways and in different amounts, depending on the situation the speakers find themselves in, and the reason or reasons they're communicating with other people.

Many cultures actually encourage men and women to talk differently and in different amounts, and these patterns for communicating are learned when men and women are young boys and girls. Children learn how to talk to other children or adults, and how to have conversations, not only from their parents, but also from their peers—other boys and girls their age. In her best-selling book, *You Just Don't Understand,* Deborah Tannen points out that although American boys and girls often play together, they spend *most* of their time playing in same-sex groups. She also points out that boys and girls *do* play some games together, but their favorite games are very often quite different. Tannen and other researchers on this topic have found that young boys, say ages eight through twelve tend to play outside the home rather than in, and they play in large groups that are hierarchically structured. The group of boys generally has a leader who tells the other boys what to do and how to do it. It is by giving orders and making the other boys play by the rules that boys achieve higher and more dominant status in the play group. Boys also achieve status by taking "center stage." They take center stage by talking a lot; they give orders and commands; they tell a lot of stories and jokes. They command attention by dominating conversations and by interrupting other boys who are speaking. The researchers also found that boys' games often have clear winners and losers and elaborate systems of rules.

Researchers found that girls play different kinds of games and abide by different rules when playing their game. In addition, girls in groups use different patterns of communication and different styles of communication when playing together. Tannen and her colleagues have found that young girls often play in small groups or in pairs. They play less often in large groups or teams outside the home. Girls' play is not so hierarchically ordered as boys' play is. In their most frequent games, like hopscotch and jump rope, every girl gets a chance to play. In many of their play activities, such as playing house, there are no "winners" or "losers." Researchers have also found that girls usually don't give many direct orders or commands to their playmates; they express their preferences as suggestions, according to Tannen. Girls often say to their playmates, "Let's do this . . . or that." Boys, on the other hand, are more direct in ordering their playmates to do this or that. Tannen is quick to point out that North American boys as well as girls want to get their way and want other children to do what they want them to do; however, boys and girls try to get their playmates to do what they want them to do in different ways.

Another well-known researcher, Marjorie Harness Goodwin, compared boys and girls engaged in two task-oriented activities. The boys were making slingshots in preparation for a fight. The girls were making jewelry; they were making rings for their fingers. Goodwin noted that the boys' activity group was hierarchically arranged. The "leader" told the other boys what to do and how to do it. The girls making the rings were more egalitarian. Everyone made suggestions about how to make the rings, and the girls tended to listen and accept the suggestions of the other girls in the group.

Goodwin is not suggesting that girls never engage in some of the communication and management behaviors boys engage in. In fact, in another study, she found that when girls play house, the girl who plays the mother gives orders to the girls who play the children. Girls seem to give orders to their peers less often than boys do when they play. The girls are practicing parent–child relationships in the game of playing house. It's very likely that when little boys play their games, they are also practicing the masculine roles they're expected to assume when they grow up.

As a result of our cultural upbringing, we learn norms of behavior and patterns of communication that are often gender based, and sometimes gender biased. We also develop stereotypes about how and how much males and females—that is, boys and girls or women and men—should, and do communicate. However, researchers have shown that many of these stereotypes actually turn out to be quite wrong.

A common stereotype that many people hold is the idea that women talk a lot, perhaps too much, and that they are always interrupting or trying to get "center stage" when someone else is talking. There is, in fact, a proverb that reinforces this idea. It states that "foxes are all tail and women are all tongue." Actually, recent research on the influence of gender on communication has shown the exact opposite to be true in many instances!

Researchers have found that men usually produce more talk than women and are more likely to interrupt another speaker than women will—particularly in public settings, such as business meetings. So although women are believed to talk more than men, study after study has shown that it is men who talk more at meetings, in mixed-group discussions, and in classrooms where girls or young women sit next to boys or young men. And this finding holds even for communicative interactions between very educated and successful professional men and women, such as professors, for example. Deborah Tannen, in her book *You Just Don't Understand*, cites a study conducted by Barbara and Gene Eakins, who tape-recorded and studied seven university faculty meetings. They found that, with one exception, men professors spoke more often and, without exception, for a longer period of time than the women professors did. The men took center stage and talked from 10.66 seconds to 17.07 seconds, while the women talked from 3 to 10 seconds, on the average. Tannen points out that the women's longest turns were still shorter than the men's shortest turns. Angela Simeone reports another example of this phenomenon in her book, *Academic Women*. She found that women professors talk at departmental meetings less often than their male colleagues do. When asked how often they spoke at departmental meetings, 46 percent of the American men professors reported that they spoke often at these meetings, but only 15 percent of the women professors reported that they spoke often at departmental meetings.

Perhaps it is our social concept of what is feminine and what is masculine that reinforces the stereotype that women talk more than men, and even causes these different patterns of communication. Maybe a woman is labeled talkative or is criticized for interrupting if she does these things at all, because our culture—as well as many cultures—teaches that women should be quiet if they want to be "feminine." Perhaps masculine culture encourages boys and men to dominate talk and to interrupt more often, and males who talk a lot and interrupt often are not criticized for doing so. These differences in the patterns of communication and styles of communicating are studied by researchers who study the effects of gender on communication. They study these effects in order to understand why misunderstandings occur between men and women in conversation. Often, it's because their styles and patterns of conversation are so different. It is important that we learn to recognize these differences so that we can learn to communicate better with people of the other gender. It is important to emphasize that these differences may be specific to North American culture. Gender can affect communication in even more and stronger ways in some other cultures. In Zulu culture, for example, a wife is forbidden to say any words that sound like the names of her father-in-law or brothers. This means that she must paraphrase these words, and she is expected to do so.

So you see, cultural differences are not the only things that affect language and communication. Language is affected by gender as well. I'm sure you can think of many ways that gender affects communication between men and women in your own culture.

Chapter 8   Gender and Communication: Male–Female Conversation as Cross-cultural Communication

🎧 B. Listening and Notetaking Script

In the last lecture, you heard about the relationship between culture and classroom communication. In this lecture, I'll talk about another variable that affects human communication. That variable is gender. Gender is the social identity that men and women learn as they grow up in a culture. For example, boys learn to be "masculine" and girls learn to be "feminine" as they grow to be men and women. Researchers have shown that men and women (and boys and girls, for that matter) communicate in quite different ways and in different amounts, depending on the situation the speakers find themselves in, and the reason or reasons they're communicating with other people.

Many cultures actually encourage men and women to talk differently and in different amounts, and these patterns for communicating are learned when men and women are young boys and girls. Children learn how to talk to other children or adults, and how to have conversations, not only from their parents, but also from their peers—other boys and girls their age. In her best-selling book, *You Just Don't Understand,* Deborah Tannen points out that although American boys and girls often play together, they spend *most* of their time playing in same-sex groups. She also points out that boys and girls *do* play some games together, but their favorite games are very often quite different. Tannen and other researchers on this topic have found that young boys, say ages eight through twelve tend to play outside the home rather than in, and they play in large groups that are hierarchically structured. The group of boys generally has a leader who tells the other boys what to do and how to do it. It is by giving orders and making the other boys play by the rules that boys achieve higher and more dominant status in the play group. Boys also achieve status by taking "center stage." They take center stage by talking a lot; they give orders and commands; they tell a lot of stories and jokes. They command attention by dominating conversations and by interrupting other boys who are speaking. The researchers also found that boys' games often have clear winners and losers and elaborate systems of rules.

Researchers found that girls play different kinds of games and abide by different rules when playing their game. In addition, girls in groups use different patterns of communication and different styles of communication when playing together. Tannen and her colleagues have found that young girls often play in small groups or in pairs. They play less often in large groups or teams outside the home. Girls' play is not so hierarchically ordered as boys' play is. In their most frequent games, like hopscotch and jump rope, every girl gets a chance to play. In many of their play activities, such as playing house, there are no "winners" or "losers." Researchers have also found that girls usually don't give many direct orders or commands to their playmates; they express their preferences as suggestions, according to Tannen. Girls often say to their playmates, "Let's do this . . . or that." Boys, on the other hand, are more direct in ordering their playmates to do this or that. Tannen is quick to point out that North American boys as well as girls want to get their way and want other children to do what they want them to do; however, boys and girls try to get their playmates to do what they want them to do in different ways.

Another well-known researcher, Marjorie Harness Goodwin, compared boys and girls engaged in two task-oriented activities. The boys were making slingshots in preparation for a fight. The girls were mak-